Your Girlfriends Only Know So Much

A Brother's Take on Dating
and Mating for Sistas

FINESSE MITCHELL

SIMON SPOTLIGHT ENTERTAINMENT
NEW YORK • LONDON • TORONTO • SYDNEY

NOTE TO READERS: Names and identifying characters of certain people portrayed have been changed. "Why Some Men Don't Call Back" and "What White Women Know About Black Men That You Don't" have been adapted from articles appearing in *Essence* magazine, February 2006 and June 2006, respectively. Used with permission.

SSE

SIMON SPOTLIGHT ENTERTAINMENT

An imprint of Simon & Schuster

1230 Avenue of the Americas, New York, New York 10020

Copyright © 2007 by Finesse Mitchell

All rights reserved, including the right of reproduction

in whole or in part in any form.

SIMON SPOTLIGHT ENTERTAINMENT and related logo

are trademarks of Simon & Schuster, Inc.

Designed by Mike Rosamilia

Manufactured in the United States of America

First Edition 10 9 8 7 6 5 4 3 2 1

Library of Congress Cataloging-in-Publication Data

Mitchell, Finesse, 1972-

Your girlfriends only know so much / Finesse Mitchell.—1st ed.

p. cm.

ISBN-13: 978-1-4169-3904-7

ISBN-10: 1-4169-3904-0

1. Man-woman relationships—United States. 2. Mate selection—United

States. 3. African American women. 4. African American men. 5.

Marriage—United States. I. Title.

HQ801.M5775 2007

646.7'708996073—dc22

2007017422

Special thanks to my inspiration,
Jessica Santos, and L.K. Mitchell, and
in loving memory of Yvette M. Dade

ACKNOWLEDGMENTS

Special thanks to all my family and friends who have supported me throughout the years. I love all of you.

Atlanta

Kate, Bill, Chris, April, Frances, and the entire Mitchell Family, especially cousins David and Cynthia; Ayanna Johnson; Joseph Brown; Zae Gilliam; Trenton Merideth; Courtney Scott; Kevin Dancy; Winston Warrior; Skip Peeples; Kevin Wright; Bo Young; Kevin Harley; Andre "Big Boi" Patten; Chase Tatum; Ryan Cameron; Zuri Stanback; Keedar Whittle; Randy Pullen; Charles Ghant; Cynthia Townsend; Leighton Condell; and April Ripley.

Los Angeles

Generate—Dave, Kara, Andy, Shukri, Terra;
Endeavor Agency—Kevin Volchok, Brian Lipson;
Chaz Foley; Howard Fishman; Jay Sloan; John Barry Whitlock; Kim Lewis; Dina Adham; Kenneth Troy Thompson; Sarah Poole; Mina Ivanova; Zalika Heart; John Cheng; QD3; Cynthia Clark; Latisha Green; Kasy Wilson;

Joel Steingold; Dondre Whitfield; Sheri Sheppard; Monica Dozier; Ryan Desouza; Roena Tapscott; Damon Lee; James Avery; Mercedes Shorte; Coki Tai; Gloria Ramos; Rand Leroy; Evan Lionel; and Marcus Guillory.

New York

Simon Spotlight Entertainment—Patrick Price and Jen Bergstrom;
My *Essence* family—Angela Burt-Murray, Lynya Floyd, Cori Murray;
My *Saturday Night Live* family;
Donald Trump (just returning the favor);
Johnny C. Taylor, Kyle Grooms, Robert Verdi, Garret Winn, JJ Ahearn, Judy, Charlie, Benny "Black" Brown;
Dr. Tanya Benenson and Dedra Tate.

Miami

Cyan, Zues, Asia, Terrell Anderson, Jodi Lawrence, Rebecca Cintron, Doyle Aaron, Janine Thompson, Jeanelle Lopez, Shella Sylla, Dayami Z., Oraine W., Nicholas "Frenchy" Suleymangil, the University of Miami, the brothers of Kappa Alpha Psi Fraternity, Inc. (especially the Iota Chi Chapter).

The book could not have been written without the brilliance of Julia Chance, and there would be no book at all without the vision and brains of my literary agent, Makila Sands (A-Town!).

CONTENTS

Introduction   xi

Chapter 1—Mirror, mirror . . .   1

Chapter 2—The List   18

Chapter 3—The Approach   36

Chapter 4—The Dating Game   65

Chapter 5—Sex: When Are Relations-Hip?   91

Chapter 6—Should You Go or Should You Stay?   115

Chapter 7—Real Love   141

Chapter 8—On Bended Knee   169

Epilogue   190

Introduction

Relationships. If you're like most women, it's a subject that's never far from the forefront of your mind. You're either fixated on how to get into one, how to improve the one you're in, or figuring out an exit plan for one that's gone bad. But if you're a *black* woman, the subject of relationships can be particularly touchy.

First of all, there's the overwhelming perception that there are not enough eligible black men to go around, and the ones who are around are too busy *getting around* to commit to one woman. And how about all of those depressing news articles, reports, and statistics describing the relationship plight of single black women? According to them, your chances of finding a boyfriend, let alone a husband, are about the same as winning the lottery or jumping into a pool headfirst after getting your hair done. It ain't happening! No wonder so many of you are distressed and anxious about your love lives.

Or perhaps, for you, it's more personal. It's not that you

can't find one, but you've already been hurt by one. Bad relationships have left you seething, pessimistic, and just plain sour on love. I can't blame you 'cause I know how some of us black men are. We meet a girl we like, tell them a couple of truths sprinkled with some lies, use their car until the transmission goes bad, ruin their credit, get them pregnant, leave them, and start dating someone they know while yelling, "How I know that's my baby?" or "You can't keep me from seeing my child!" I mean, let's be real; it's no coincidence that several of you have just thrown up your hands and declared, "Jesus is my boyfriend!" You haven't been touched by the spirit; you're just fed up with us.

But don't count us out just yet. I am here to tell you that there are plenty of good brothas out here who are gainfully employed; have decent credit; occupy a church pew for more than just weddings, funerals, and Easter; and know how to treat women. They just haven't been marketed very well, and you haven't been equipped with the tools to help you know the difference between Mr. Right and Mr. Very, Very Wrong. You need a man's advice. You need to get a black man's perspective on black men. That's where this book comes in.

I'm best-known as a comedian and actor, starting my career on BET's *Comic View,* and then as a cast member on *Saturday Night Live* for three seasons. For those of you who've only experienced my sidesplitting sense of humor, you're probably thinking, *He's funny and all, but what can he possibly tell me about finding a good man and having a fulfilling relationship?* That's totally understandable. I'm not a psychologist or a licensed therapist. What makes me qualified to give you advice? For starters, I'm a black man. I'm more than thirty years old, a college graduate, and in a committed relationship. And ever since I got my first serious girlfriend, I've become somewhat of an authority on dating and relationships to my single, black, female friends. Up until that time I had a bit of a reputation for . . . Well, let's just say, being the opposite of commitment. My single friends wanted to know what made me finally settle down and commit to one woman. More important, they wanted me to help them figure men out. They are great women and have lots going for them, yet finding Mr. Right just wasn't happening.

I didn't mind giving them advice, because I know how hard it can be out there for sisters. However, I noticed they would seek my advice *after* the damage was done. They would consult their girlfriends first, and consequently screw up a situation with a man that could have been easily fixed or avoided. Now don't get me wrong. Women successfully advise one another on tons of stuff, like hairstyles, makeup, exercise, jobs, clothes, etc. But asking a woman a question about a man is about as helpful as bringing a box of Krispy Kreme donuts to a Weight Watchers meeting.

Women need to ask *men* about men. And not experts, either. Experts sound pretty smart because they're always using catchy phrases, like "connect with your authentic self" or "a big ego is a no-no." But does anyone truly understand all that psychobabble? You need straightforward information that's not only going to tell you the truth about black men and relationships, but also let you in on the things that only men know about men.

Like you, I have had my share of dating drama and less-than-ideal relationships. Because I'm a man, I'm well-aware of the games we play. And because I'm a son, a brother, and a friend to women, I understand how our games impact you. Most of all, I truly believe black men and women can have positive relationships if we take the time to understand one another.

I also wrote this book because I *love* black women. I love y'all like red Kool-Aid and spending other people's money. When I was a boy, my dream was to marry the Palmer's Cocoa Butter lady in the ads I saw in *Ebony* magazine. Later, I had major crushes on my two babysitters, Monica and Angie. By the time I started growing peach fuzz under my chin, I wanted Whitney Houston—the old Whitney. The Clive Davis–discovered, Arista-records, "Saving All My Love for You" Whitney. Then I wanted Janet Jackson the moment I saw "The Pleasure Principle" video, with her dressed all in black, wearing Guess jeans and kneepads. Later it became "That's the Way Love Goes" Janet, followed by Superbowl-Sunday Janet, with those . . . Um, where was I? Oh yeah, I love black women. Robin Givens before Mike Tyson; Vanity—enough said! Lisa Bonet from *A Different World*, Jada Pinkett from *A Different World*, and Halle Berry from *any* world.

Given my love for black women, it's hard for me to sit back and watch the big mistakes you all make when it comes to us black men. With that in mind, I want to give you some insight on where we stand on the whole dating-and-relationship game. Maybe if I can help you to understand us a little better, I can single-handedly save the black family. Okay, okay, that may be a bit much. But at the very least I might be able to get a handful of women to stop blaming men for ruining their lives when they knew from the jump that the guy was no good, crazy, or still living with his momma with no desire to move.

Consider this book a gentlemen's guide just for women. I'll teach you how to meet, date, and have a successful relationship with the man of your dreams—Well, kind of. Remember, I'm a comedian, not a miracle worker. But this book is filled with practical suggestions; some of my own crazy dating adventures; and fun quizzes, diagrams, and charts for you to study, because there's a comprehensive test at the end of the book. Just joking. Maybe hearing one black man's point of view might help you make sense of the nonsense that makes sense only to men. Does that make sense? At the very least, you will smile and laugh throughout my book. I am confident of that. Hell, making people laugh is the second best thing I do.

You listen to your girlfriends all the time when it comes to figuring out your man or future man, but you also should be listening to me. Because when it comes to black men, your girlfriends only know so much.

CHAPTER ONE

mirror, mirror . . .

"Mirror, Mirror on the wall,

who's the jazziest chick walking the mall?

Every time I ask, you always say ME,

and if that's the truth, Mirror, then where's my PC?!

I'm not talking computers or being politically correct.

I'm talking about Prince Charming; should I put you in check?

My good stuff needs global warming, and did I forget to mention

my mother wants a grandbaby, and my intellect needs attention?

Do I need to remind you how patient I've been with this game?

Each day you say my man is coming, but each day ends the same.

So stop stalling, eye-balling, and reflect something new.

Show me his photo, his address—Hell, a first name will do."

"Hold on, baby girl (he's a ghetto mirror), *don't roll your eyes at me.*

Everyday you look at yourself, and I tell you what I see.

You beautiful, you smart, you the no limit AmEx card.

You motivated, you sharp—and your 'milkshake brings all the boys to the yard.'

You look at me with attitude, like I don't bring men your way.

You said the first guy was too short. The last guy 'looked' gay.

And all the guys in between, you said were too broke or too nice.

I brought you the single schoolteacher, but you wanted the rapper with a wife.

I agree, Mike is a weed head and Dwayne is way too chatty.

Granted, Rick is single now, but he's also your best friend's baby daddy.

I brought you the NBA athlete, but you cried foul when he was never home.

So next I brought you righteous Raheem, but you couldn't leave that pork alone.

Then there was Christian Chris, but he lived with his momma.

There was jovial Joel, but you said he looked like Osama.

Everytime I find you the next Barak Obama,

You go chase some L.A. actor who only lives for drama.

And Jamaican James was cool as a tropical breeze,

But you instantly claimed he had O.J. tendencies.

Hey, I finally know what your problem be,

So let me break it down easy, for you to see:

Before a man can love you the way you deserve,

You have to put aside your desires and work up the nerve

To look within.

"In other words, Boo,

Before I can help find the One, you must first find you."

It's a simple truth: Before you can begin to know what kind of mate or relationship you want, it helps to have some sense of who you are. It may seem like a no-brainer, but based on the sheer number of TV shows, syndicated radio programs, books and magazine articles dedicated to relationship issues—not to mention a select group of grown-ass women clamoring for the affection of Flavor Flav—self-evaluation is a basic step that many people are skipping.

A mate is supposed to enhance your life, not fill in all the gaps. Remember that line from the film *Jerry Maguire*, when Tom Cruise tells Renée Zellweger, "You complete me"? Well, that has to be the dumbest line I've ever heard. Complete yourself! Another dumb one is, "I can't breath without you." Oh really, now? If that were the case, every time a couple broke up there'd be a bunch of dead folks lying around. Before you get all caught up in some high-speed cat-and-mouse chase with a man, you have to get to know yourself and feel comfortable in your own skin. That means knowing the basics about you.

Who are you?

And before you start describing how you look; rattling down the list of your accomplishments; stating whose child, mother, or sibling you are; or listing all your possessions, take a moment to really think about who you are—*minus* the various accouterments, labels, and notions that you or others may let define you. It's not that those things aren't important, but they're the enhancers, not the true you.

So, *who* are you? What are your beliefs and convictions?

What are you passionate about? What are your values? Are you religious? Are you an atheist? Do you put a premium on book smarts or street savvy? What do like to do for fun and leisure? Are you high maintenance? High strung? Or can you just relax and go with the flow? Do you always put the cheapest gas in your car? Are you always in the streets or more of a homebody? Do you like kids? Do you like other people's kids? Hell, do you like your own kids? If you met a guy with kids, would that be cool with you? Are you short-tempered or patient? Are you a control freak whose mantra is "My way or the highway"? Are you a people person or a loner? What do you want out of life? These are the types of questions you must ask yourself and answer honestly in order to be realistic about who you are. Moreover, you have to love and accept yourself—flaws and all. That doesn't mean there's no room for growth, but you first have to have a clear understanding of what needs improving.

ARE YOU READY TO DATE? ·

1) You refer to your ex-boyfriend as:
   a. "Mr. Wrong-for-Me."
   b. "the liar and the cheat."
   c. "my man"—because things ain't over until you say they are over.
   d. "my ex" or his name.

4

2) If you suddenly see your ex-boyfriend, you:
   a. start searching for the knife that you keep in your purse for these kinds of occasions.
   b. give him a polite nod or hello, and keep it moving.
   c. immediately go in the opposite direction no matter how long it takes you out of your way.

3) Your idea of planning for the future is:
   a. a savings account and a 401(K) plan.
   b. "What future?"—you believe in living for today.
   c. the weekly lottery ticket you purchase from the 7-Eleven.
   d. marrying well.

4) The man you call the most is:
   a. the pizza man.
   b. your maintenance man.
   c. your dad, grandfather, brother, or gay best friend.

5) Your idea of a perfect date is:
   a. Sunday visiting hours at the penitentiary.
   b. dinner and a movie.
   c. reviewing your date's credit report.

6) Which song would best describe how you act when you are in a relationship?
   a. "Dangerously in Love"
   b. "You're Gonna Love Me"
   c. "Ordinary People"

7) "All men are _____."
   a. dogs
   b. liars
   c. different

8) Your favorite stress release is:
   a. exercise.
   b. sticking needles into a voodoo doll of your
      ex-boyfriend.
   c. sex.
   d. eating.

9) What you find most attractive in a man is his:
   a. bank account.
   b. job.
   c. personality.
   d. physique.

10) You currently have:
   a. a restraining order against you.
   b. a child that is nursing.
   c. no job, no money, and no prospects.
   d. none of the above.

ANSWER KEY

   1) a-1, b-2, c-3, d-1
   2) a-3, b-1, c-2
   3) a-1, b-2, c-3, d-3
   4) a-3, b-2, c-1
   5) a-3, b-2, c-2
   6) a-2, b-3, c-1
   7) a-3, b-2, c-1
   8) a-1, b-3, c-2, d-3
   9) a-3, b-2, c-1, d-2
   10) a-3, b-3, c-3, d-1

If you scored:

26–30 Stop, Do Not Pass Go!
Go to therapy, join a 12-step program, go to church, or do *something*. But do *not* date. You're nowhere near ready.

16–25 Almost But Not Quite
You can read a few self-help books (this book counts) and try again in a few days.

10–15 Get Out There Already!
What are you waiting for?

Some of you allow a relationship to totally overtake you. It completely defines you. Once you enter it, it's like you lose yourself and become an extension of him. Suddenly you're down to go anywhere he likes to go for fun. All of his friends are now your friends. You dress the way he likes you to dress. You watch the television shows and movies he likes to watch. His favorite sports team is your favorite sports team, which is strange 'cause you don't even like sports. You never raised a barbell, but because he likes to work out, you sign up for the deluxe gym package that you abandon after one week. Hell, I even know a woman who *never, ever* smoked weed, but because her man indulged, she became a blunt-roller extraordinaire!

I, like a lot of men, actually love it when a woman becomes an extension of her man—to a point. If we wanted to date ourselves, we'd never come out of those long, hot, relaxing showers we like so much.

If a guy becomes your entire world and you two break up, you'll have no clue who you are or what to do next. In fact, people at the clubs will still call you K-Mac's girl, because that's the *only thing* they ever knew about you. You wouldn't believe how many women leave every aspect of their own lives up to their man, and when he's gone, they're lost and have the toughest time moving on. Those are the types you hear about, who key their ex-boyfriends' cars or wait in the bushes for them to show up somewhere with their new women, so they can jump out and throw rocks. They simply can't remember who they are without their exes. Consequently, they've lost themselves *and* their minds.

Now don't get me wrong, I know some men do the type of dirt that makes women want to destroy property, step to them, or worse. But no matter how satisfied a wronged woman may feel immediately after pulling some scandalous stunt on an ex-lover, I've never heard anyone say that they truly felt better in the long run. The temporary satisfaction of revenge is just that: temporary. All that plotting and drama is never a guarantee that you'll win a man back, or get even after a man's wronged you. On top of that, you just might find yourself with a police record before it's all over. Next thing you know, he's telling everybody he left you, because you were nuts. Acting out is never worth it.

MEN LOVE TO SAY SHE'S CRAZY ·············

Dear ladies,

Black men love to say you are crazy if you do or say anything that resembles crazy. Sometimes we do it only to convince ourselves that our childish and immature behavior is normal, so no fault or blame lies with us. But other times, it's you! Boy, I have stories that would make you want to shake a grown woman by the shoulders and yell, "What were you thinking?" No one likes for crazy to unexpectedly jump out and start tap dancing. We do not care how you got to that state of mind. If you know you are not in the correct state of mind to meet any men, take all the time you need to get better.

It is a proven fact that men make unstable women absolutely crazy. Even the most perfectly sane woman can go bonkers because of the actions of a man. And yes, slashing tires, throwing bricks through windows, and repeatedly calling his job, pretending to be a very irate hooker that he ran out on without paying the night before, all count as crazy! This entire book could be filled from cover to cover with what-he-did-to-me stories (which is my sequel, so don't get any bright ideas), but it is still crazy.

Do yourself a favor and fix crazy before you start to date. A lot of women think they need a new man to help them get over the old man that drove them nuts. Big mistake. Men can detect when something is not right and pull away, leaving you more disgusted with men or more brokenhearted. Even the nicest and most considerate man in the world cannot fix crazy, and his first instinct is to bail out and save himself before he gets too invested.

Again, fix crazy first, then come holla!

Love,

Finesse

Perhaps this extreme scenario doesn't fully apply to you. Yet, on some level, you may still be losing parts of yourself for the sake of attracting a man or being in a relationship. Maybe you're defining yourself and your happiness solely on the attention you get from men. Or you could be buying into some misguided notions of what you are supposed to be based on things your girlfriend or grandmomma told you, or what you saw in your favorite romantic movie. Either way you're not being true to who you are and what you need. *Do not* fall down that black hole.

In some cases esteem is the issue. Some sisters have self-love issues, because they were raised in families where love wasn't always exhibited in healthy ways. They may have experienced dysfunction, neglect, or even abuse. Maybe love was conditional and only shown when certain criteria were met. Perhaps love was displayed with material things to the detriment of emotional needs. Or maybe real love just wasn't felt on a consistent basis.

When looking back on a less than ideal childhood you have to realize you can't change it. Acknowledge it, glean whatever lessons you can from it, and try your best to move on. It might sound easier said than done, but it's necessary in order for you to heal. And what you do to heal is totally up to you. Maybe it's consulting with a therapist, counselor, or minister. Some of you may find comfort from calling on whatever higher power you rely on to get you through. Talking to a good friend might be helpful, or a very old person if you have time for a story that starts with, "Back in the day, right after the Great Depression, nobody had much but one another. . . ."

You might even try talking to kids, because their advice is always simple and straight to the point. Check out this scenario that I've titled "Get Over It":

Get Over It ·····························

You and a kid are in a park on the swings, going back and forth. Both of you come to a stop about the same time and just sit there contemplating life.

> You: My mom hated me and used to beat me for
>   no reason.
> Kid: Mine too. Hey, let's go get some ice cream!

What the kid is really saying: "Big deal, girl. At least you're grown and can do what you want. I still get beat every day and will probably continue to for some time to come. Now stop crying about yesterday and take me to get some damn ice cream before my momma sees I'm missing!"

All I'm saying is don't waste time wallowing in past hurts. Get what you need, and proceed.

One of the beauties of adulthood is that we don't have to stay in childhood situations that weren't good for us. When I think about it, my woman could be a prime candidate for self-love issues. She adored her dad, and he could do no wrong in her eyes, even though he was hardly ever around. She found out as a teenager the reason he was MIA: He had multiple families around the country. No kidding. What amazes me, though, is how she never talks about her dad in a bad way. In fact, she actually jokes and laughs about how clever he was to pull off his multiple-family act for so long, undiscovered.

Now, for her *mother* it's probably a different story. I get the sense that Ma Dukes is probably still a bit miffed at that ol' dude, but my girl only focuses and thinks of the good times long gone. She talks about missing him, but she also tells me funny stories about things that happened when he was home. And as far as I can tell, she is not bitter, she is not scarred, and she does not have abandonment issues like you might expect, considering I have a career that keeps me on the road a lot. When it comes to her dad, she only wishes they got to spend more time together, since he passed away not too long ago. For my part, I tell her all the time that I love her and that she is beautiful, just in case she didn't hear it enough from her dad.

A lot about our self-esteem is shaped by the people we choose to surround us. Long before some man gets a chance to throw a little hate your way, you may already receive it from friends or even family members. Hurtful words or actions from the people nearest and dearest to you can inflict major damage. It's imperative that you recognize the haters in your inner circle and immediately cut them off, even if they are family.

I know, blood is thicker than water, but sometimes it's just a thick mess! Some of your loved ones may not like you (or themselves for that matter), so why pretend for the sake of family? We can't help whom we're related to, but there is no law that says you have to let relatives mentally beat you down like a piñata. Be cordial with them at family reunions, weddings, and funerals, and keep it moving. If you can help it, keep your distance—like a couple of states—from negative family members.

In the case of friends, know that some of them have their own demons that they are battling, some of them unbeknownst to you. They'll have you believing you're the problem when it's really them. Don't be afraid to take a long break from those types. Trust me, you'll be just fine without them.

And while I'm on the subject of self-worth, I have to say that our society at large has not always done a good job of affirming the black woman's image. The Euro beauty standards that are so prevalent in our culture have many black women feeling very insecure about their appearances. They truly don't think they're beautiful. Considering the mostly white faces that grace magazine covers, the lack of television shows or big-screen flicks with nonwhite women holding it down, and the abundance of bootylicious bodies in rap videos, it's hard *not* to feel inadequate. (I strongly believe the growth juice they are injecting in chickens to make them bigger has many of our Popeye's and Church's Chicken–eating young women growing up and developing way too quickly. Hell, a lot of them look ready at age twelve to be in a Lil John video!) Then there are the high-profile brothers and their love for pink toes (white girls), but, hey, that's a topic for another chapter, or another book.

No wonder I hear my single girlfriends say they feel like they are last on the black man's social totem pole. I definitely see where they're coming from. In fact, I tell my white girl all the time that my single black sisters have it just as bad as she does out here. Just kidding, calm down! That was a joke. My girl isn't white, she's Asian. They're jokes! Okay, that was the last one.

I wouldn't call it a conspiracy, but there is definitely some brainwashing going on. I'm reminded of that every time I hear comments, like, "She's pretty for a dark-skinned girl." As if, to be pretty *and* dark is some rare fluke. Too many of us have subscribed to the mainstream's idea of what beauty is, and it's a shame.

And I'll admit it: Some of us black men can be the worst perpetrators of this kind of self-hate. I've seen brothers on the streets or in the club who are guilty of focusing only on some HalleBerry-Beyoncé-Lo while totally ignoring the sexy-ass Fantasias of the world. Or there are the dudes who get a little too distracted by aggressive white women who step to them in nightclubs, buying them pricey dark liquor, wearing tight jeans (they've obviously been eating Popeye's and Church's fried chicken too!) and dancing *on* beat. It's just confusing for us . . . um, them, the black man. Or so I've heard.

"Black is beautiful!" I used to hear that all the time growing up, along with "Black don't crack; it ages gracefully." And later on, "Crack is whack!" But I digress. What I'm getting at here is you can't allow the images you see in the media to define your beauty. You come in a range of complexions, shapes, and sizes—all of which are lovely. And if a man you like can't appreciate your unique beauty, he ain't worth your time.

Confidence is very sexy. In fact, to me, sexy goes hand in hand with confidence. If you're not a confident person, there's no way you can be sexy. Cute, maybe, but not sexy. We men can spot a confident woman a mile away. She's the one who walks with her head held high, looks you directly in the eye when you're having a conversation, and knows how to assert herself without being overly aggressive. She's putting her best foot forward rather than being preoccupied by any self-perceived shortcomings or flaws. She's not letting anything hold her back from seizing opportunities or jumping in the spotlight. Most of all, she doesn't appear desperate or insecure.

Confidence is a strength that people flock to. I've often heard women say that when they're feeling confident, that's when they usually meet a man—and they may not have even been looking for one!

Think of it this way: When out in the world, we are like a piece of art putting ourselves on display. We want to attract only those who see and appreciate our unique and special beauty. Most of all, when we find *the One*, we hope to make the kind of impression that will assure we will be loved and treasured for a long time to come.

If you find yourself continuously frustrated about the types of admirers attracted to your art, maybe it's time to check your canvas. If you look in the mirror and don't see what's so uniquely special, your canvas is blank! Embrace your individuality. Break out the brushes and paint. Use bright colors, bold strokes, interesting shapes and textures! Heck, add some birds and trees if you like. Why? Because with every brush stroke, you get to know yourself a little better. And that's what it's about—who you are. Trust me, the more you know about yourself, the harder it is for guys to run game on you.

My little sister once asked me, "Why do guys like one girl one minute and then someone else the next? And don't tell me anything about paint and brushes—come with the real talk this time, playa!"

Did I mention that she's a smart, boy-crazy, suburban queen?

I broke it down to her the best I could, but not before putting the focus back on her. I told her, "You have to get to know who you are and find things that make you happy outside of boys, so that when there are no boys around, you won't freak out and not know what to do with yourself." I'm offering up that same advice to you, and we aren't even related. As you search for your Mr. McDreamy, proceed with a healthy degree of self-love, confidence, and common sense. And remember, the more you know you, the better you will be in a relationship with someone else.

CHAPTER TWO

FINESSE'S TOP-TEN LIST FOR THE FUTURE MRS. MITCHELL
(in no particular order)

··

1) Fine
2) Likes to cook
3) Funny
4) Caring
5) Outgoing
6) Trustworthy
7) Smart/Common sense
8) Confident
9) Spiritual
10) Good work ethic (slackers need not apply)

Throughout the years I've heard just about every woman I know speak about her list. At first I assumed they were referring to groceries or what they wanted for Christmas. My mom even had a list, but hers was more of a *hit* list. As I got older and wiser to the ways of women, or, more specifically, tried to date Linda T. in the ninth grade, I learned that *the list* was actually an inventory of the characteristics and qualities that women desire in their future husbands. When I made my move on Linda, she stuck her list in my locker. After reading it, I soon realized that I only possessed two of the twenty qualities she required. "Handsome." Check. "Funny and not conceited." Yep, that's me! "Nice grade of hair." Umm . . .

That day after school I immediately bought a Fabulaxer perm kit, with hopes that acquiring good hair overnight would be one more thing on her list that I possessed. But her other requirements, like "must be good in algebra" and "must have a convertible Volkswagen," weren't such an easy fix.

Although I didn't make the cut, according to Linda's list, that experience taught me that *the list* is something that women take very seriously. Why? Because it's a constant reminder of what they want—or don't want—in a man. Whether they meticulously write it in a diary, simply jot their prerequisites on a sheet of notebook paper, or just keep a running tally in their heads, the list gives them one of the most powerful tools you can possess in the dating game: a sense of clarity. Some women even get real creative with their lists, giving them catchy names, like "Mate Must-Haves" or "My Future Huzbin." Nowadays some women are just happy with a list titled "My Future Baby Daddy." You know who you are, but let's not go there.

I know a woman from Philly named Aisha whose dating philosophy is "variety is the spice of life." She is a modern, free-spirited type who prides herself on her ability to attract and date different kinds of men. Yet she was constantly frustrated by her inability to develop an exclusive, long-lasting relationship. Inevitably her assortment of potential Mr. Rights were always wrong for her. I asked her if she had a list. She looked at me like I had three heads. "Of course!" she said. "It's a list of every man who didn't work out."

"I'm referring to your future-man list, woman!" She wrinkled up her nose and looked the other way as if my breath smelled like wet feet in tube socks.

"Fin," she said, laughing, "you sound like a throwback from the fifties with that list crap." In her mind, having the type of list I was speaking of meant she'd be limiting her options and imposing an agenda on a man, both of which seemed very old-school to her. After she'd experienced a particularly devastating breakup, I felt it was high time that she gained some focus, so I broke it down to her. Here's what I told Aisha, and I think it's pretty good advice for you too.

Having a list is beneficial for the following reasons: It keeps you from settling for less-than-desirable situations, it can eliminate a lot of unnecessary drama from your love life, and you're not wasting your time—or ours for that matter—on a relationship that hasn't got a snowball's chance in hell of surviving. Think about it like this: If you had a choice of picking out a free car and you could choose any car in the world, I seriously doubt that you would jump up and down screaming, "Dodge Neon!"

This time Aisha got what I was saying. She realized that having some advance idea of what she wanted in a man didn't limit her options—it actually fined-tuned the dating process. She also learned that having an agenda isn't a bad thing, either. It's empowering. *Not* having an agenda is what's really old-school, because it puts you in the position of passively accepting and tolerating whatever comes your way. Once Aisha got her list going, she started dating smarter.

On the Real

My fifteen-year-old sister showed me her list of everything her ideal guy had to have before he could date her. When I saw her farfetched prerequisites, like "must have light brown eyes," "should have cute guy friends for my girlfriends to date," "should have a job at Burger King or Pizza Hut, so we can roll there anytime and get the hook up," and "needs to have two thousand songs on his iPod," I immediately pulled out a pen, so we could make some revisions.

Like my sister's list, some women base theirs on pure fantasy. Usually, the younger they are, the longer and more imaginative their lists. I know young ladies who include exhaustive details, all the way down to seat warmers in a man's BMW. Damn! Now a brotha's Beamer has to have seat warmers?

Luckily, as women mature, they gain wisdom about the things that really matter and sidestep those that don't. They revise their lists and make a couple of cuts. Curly hair gets tossed out the window, hazel-colored eyes are no longer a must, and a fancy car with spinning rims and TV screens attached to the rear bumper are now considered a bad investment. Characteristics, such as being considerate, thoughtful, employed, and reliable soon jump to the top of the list, right before "must be noticeably taller than me." Women will hold onto the height thing for as long as they can. In a nutshell, they realize that Superman simply does not exist, so their list becomes less superficial and more practical.

There's a woman I know who I'll call Cinnamon (no, she's not a stripper!). She's a nurse in Los Angeles who's attractive, fine, smart, and presently single. She crafted a no-nonsense list of her ideal man's qualities that looked like this:

1) Must be a man of God
2) Has to be successful in the business world
3) Has to be tall, good-looking, faithful, mature, over thirty years old, no kids, and never been married
4) No bisexuals
5) Has to be well-spoken, well-dressed; hip and not nerdy
6) Should be well-endowed, good in bed, attentive, affectionate, romantic, fun, and exciting
7) Most important of all, there will be no conflicts between us

Like I said in the previous chapter, it's great when a woman knows what things she absolutely has to have in a man before she even considers him a candidate for the "interview process." So on the surface Cinnamon's list looked good. She'd covered several bases, from the type of work her mate would have, to his sense of spirituality, to the attention she wanted him to give her. But had Cinnamon truly considered the reality of her desires? Let's weigh the facts.

A God-fearing man is always a plus—submitting to a higher power keeps you humble and grounded. And Cinnamon's wish for a successful businessman is cool, but there are varying levels of success. She could have a man who's a middle-management type, who's home for dinner every night. Or she could have a large-and-in-charge type— think Donald Trump, Russell Simmons, or Steve Jobs—who works long hours, attends all kinds of social functions throughout the week, and has to travel frequently. The latter may not have the time or energy to fulfill those other mandates on her list—like being affectionate, attentive, and romantic, not to mention burning up the bedroom. Most professional men and women whose job requires a lot of brainpower and stress will tell you, *"We be tired!"* Also, a driven man who knows he has his stuff together may be arrogant or have a pompous, condescending attitude. Sometimes ambition and self-centeredness are very close cousins.

Let's face it: The more attractive a man is and the more money he makes, the more he's considered a catch. He knows it, you know it, and some white women let him know *they* know it. It takes a secure woman to handle the attention that this type of man will undoubtedly receive from other women, especially if that attention becomes disrespectful toward her. Also, since some successful men feel that they can have their pick of women, infidelity could become an issue in the relationship, no matter how God fearing he claims to be. I don't know if Cinnamon is truly up for all that.

Then there's that part about him being over thirty, never married with no children. Now, I'm no statistician, but the older a man is, the more likely he is to have been married or have a Travonté, Madison, or Mistakalina running around somewhere. Lastly, that bit about there being no conflicts between them is a total fantasy. It's like saying you'll never go to bed angry. It's a nice sentiment, but it's just not true. Even the most loving couples who've been together for years have gone to bed with ill thoughts, and I'll just leave it at that. Just because something's settled in the moment doesn't mean it's resolved. It just means you've agreed to disagree for the sake of not going to jail, so you might as well get some sleep.

I'm not saying that Cinnamon shouldn't aim high in order to get what she feels she deserves, and I'm definitely not trying to discourage her or any other woman who thinks this list is reasonable. But my goal is to tell you women the truth about men from a man's point of view. Does Cinnamon deserve a man like the one on her list? Hell yeah! Is there a man out there who fits her list to a tee? Sure. I know of at least thirty who fit the bill, and they are all good men. Yet some of the women who dated them, thinking that they had their ideal man, learned very quickly that some of the conflicting issues I mentioned were deal breakers. They landed a successful man, but weren't prepared to deal with the compromises that come with that type of lifestyle. Cinnamon has a great list, but she needs to be aware of what her desires entail.

Currently, Cinnamon is thirty years old, very hopeful, and still very single.

A Little Flexibility Goes a Long Way ·············

It's smart to keep your list flexible, because you never know what other factors could come into play. My friend Trina, twenty-six years old, is a fine example of what I'm talking about. After a series of less-than-ideal relationships, she dubbed her list "Trina's Top Man-Priorities." It read like this:

1) Has to have a job
2) Has to have a car
3) Must be attractive
4) Has to have a great relationship with his mother
5) Must have common sense

Now, Trina doesn't have any particular order of importance for these must-haves on her list, but she said the guy she dates must have these five simple things *in order* for her to strongly consider him a candidate for her affections. By the way, Trina had one of the shortest lists of all the women I interviewed, aside from my mom whose list simply read "black and breathing!"

Eventually Trina met Derek, twenty-nine years old, through a mutual friend. She thought he was good-looking. He had a nice car and often spoke affectionately of his mother. He dressed nice, smelled good, and was always on time for their dates. Trina really liked Derek, but guess what? Derek didn't have a job. He was laid off two weeks before he met Trina and was currently going on interviews for a new gig. Trina learned this during their first telephone conversation, when they had a chance to speak at length. Even though she didn't get a vote of confidence from her girls, who constantly chirped, "Girl, he ain't got no job!" Trina found Derek to be very optimistic. He had good energy, and so far, money hadn't been an issue between them.

Soon Trina realized she needed to revise her list to accommodate the reality of her situation. She hadn't dated for a while, and she was lonely. She could either stay true to her list, or go out for dinner and a movie. She didn't wait for Derek to get a job before they got too involved and said she felt stupid thinking she should. Instead she just went for it, because, as she put it, "He was so nice and so funny, and Trina ain't getting no younger."

I heard from one of her close friends that they are still dating, and although it took several months, Derek found a job.

The lesson here is that you should be committed to what's on your wish list, but remember you can't date it. Life in general is unpredictable, and people in particular have complexities that no list can capture or predict. Say you had your heart set on marrying a high roller, but instead of landing a banker, you landed a baker. He's moving muffins instead of municipal funds, but he is good at what he does, enjoys his gig, brings home the bread, and keeps you more than satisfied. Maybe you don't want to date a man with kids, but you'll never know how you honestly feel until you meet a man you really like with a child or children. You may say, "I will never date a man who has a criminal record"—until you realize all those questionable gifts he gives you look great in your apartment.

THE MALE DATEABILITY FLOW CHART

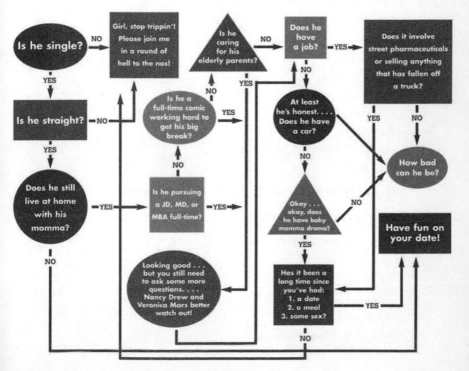

Devising Your List ································

Whether you realize it or not, you probably started your list when you were a little girl. I think women are raised believing that relationships are eminent, so y'all start planning early. You dreamed of your future husband and wrote out baby names, like Sidney, Asher, Jasmine, Davarsious, and Sincere, for the children you hope to have together. Maybe you delighted in Cinderella-type fairy tales where it was all about landing the prince who would come in and sweep you off your feet to take you where you'd both live happily ever after. Back then, if you wrote your list down, it might have read something like this:

1) Handsome
2) Nice
3) Handsome
4) Strong
5) Handsome
6) Brave
7) Handsome

By the time you hit high school you realized that a guy who is simply handsome, brave, and strong wasn't going to cut it, so you made some revisions:

1) Cute
2) Dresses nice
3) Good kisser
4) Has a driver's license

5) Great dancer
6) Can buy me cool gifts
7) Handsome

Chances are your early ideas of the perfect man had more to do with physical and material attributes than anything else. That's understandable. Those are the things that impressed you when you were young. Physical attractiveness may still be a draw for you, but now that you're a grown woman, you should know all that glitters isn't gold. There are many Adonises out there, but you need more than a man with good looks to sustain a healthy, successful relationship.

When I was in elementary school, half the girls I knew wanted to marry Michael Jackson and had every boy buying penny loafers and trying to moonwalk. But today, how many black women do you know actually want to marry Michael Jackson, even without his financial problems and children with names like Blanket and who wear masks?

In the first chapter we focused on defining who you are. By now I hope that you've seriously assessed your characteristics and personality traits, because doing that will help you come up with the list for your ideal mate. I've told you about the various ways women I know do their lists, but how you keep track of *your* list is up to you. I highly recommend that you begin this process by writing it out. It's like when you practiced spelling words in grade school. Putting those words down on paper helped to solidify them in your mind, and got you better prepared for the test. (Writing them out on a small piece of paper cupped tightly in my hand always worked for me.) Anyway, it can work the same way for your list. But don't obsess over it *too much*. Most important, don't let your list become a crutch. You don't need to carry it around with you to pull out every time you meet someone you're interested in. And don't have it tattooed on your arm either, because revisions can get expensive.

When you think about the qualities you'd like in a man, sometimes a good place to start is with men you like and admire. Maybe it is an uncle who always treats your aunt like a queen, a neighbor with impeccable manners, a family friend who is a dapper dresser, or that intelligent guy who was your science partner in college. If no good men readily come to mind, because the last few dudes you dated left you feeling hurt, angry, or bitter, use those negative experiences to your benefit. What you may not realize is that even the no-good, trifling guys you've encountered have left you closer to figuring out what you want and need in a partner. They made you extremely aware of what you *don't* want, so you can begin your list by writing the things you won't tolerate from the next guy. Just because you attract the same type of man again and again doesn't mean you have to date them. Sometimes it's as simple as recognizing that this is a road full of potholes you have been down before, so make a U-turn and speed up.

Now, let's start your list. Begin by daydreaming about your ideal man. What does he look like? Is he a suit-wearing professional or the hard-working blue-collar type? Does he aspire to the finer things in life, or are his tastes a little more basic? Does he have good credit, a 401(K) plan, and health insurance? Does he love his mother and live in his own house? Does he want kids? Does he know how to cook? Is he great in bed? Does he believe in the important stuff, like God, marriage, and car insurance? Would you like him to be openly affectionate toward you, or would you prefer he be more discrete? Is it important that he socialize with your friends and family?

As you write down all of these wishful qualities, ask yourself why they are important to you. For example, is your desire for a guy who's built like a linebacker because you like a man who is in shape, or is it rooted in a deeper need you have to feel physically safe? Do you want someone who's financially set, because you don't feel you could accomplish the same on your own? Examine your motives, because sometimes the cover of the book might not look like something you'd be interested in, but once you open it up you realize it's exactly what you were looking for. Ideally you want to come into a relationship whole. It's not healthy or fair to look to a mate to fulfill your inadequacies and shortcomings.

There are no hard and fast rules for your list. It can be long or short, basic or detailed. But the key in making the list work is for you to be true to who you are and true about what you want. If you compromise what's on your list, understand why you did so and take full responsibility for the consequences if things don't work out. I hate to hear women complain, "I don't know why I got involved with him in the first place." Yes, you do. You compromised. So stop egging his house and keying his car. Move on! Or better yet, maybe you should egg your own house and key your own car every time you get yourself into a situation that you knew was a bad idea from the start. You'll learn.

The 80/20 Rule

Now, what if you had this dream man all to yourself, but he wasn't as romantic as you'd like him to be? Perhaps he's thoughtful and calls all the time, but his work often keeps him on the road? How about if he wasn't totally your physical type, but he treated you real nice? What if he was most of the things you wanted, but, for some reason, something was missing? What would you be satisfied with?

If you find yourself in this type of situation, it's time to employ what I call the 80/20 Rule: If you meet somebody with 80 percent of what you are looking for, by all means pay attention to what's in front of you. Don't miss out on the love of your life because you're holding out for 20 percent of what may not even be important in the long run. Determine the qualities and traits that are hands down, absolutely nonnegotiable. These should account for your 80 percent. Qualities that may not be your ideal, but are things you can certainly live with, should make up the remaining 20 percent. If you want a nonsmoker, there's no negotiating that he'll only smoke when he's not in your presence. If he's honest, respects you, makes you laugh, and takes care of business in the bedroom, but isn't as fashionable as you'd like, you can always shop for him.

If you hate drama, guns, inconsistency, weed smoke, strip joints, eating at Waffle House at 4 a.m. or being around a bunch of dudes who aren't gainfully employed and always start and end their sentences with the N-word, don't date a drug dealer. If you hate working out and eating right, don't date a body builder. If you love to go swimming in the ocean, skydiving, bungee jumping, and hanging out at the library, but you hate PlayStation and Xbox, don't date a black man between the ages of eighteen and thirty-eight. I'm serious! And if you love to laugh, but hate paying for everything, don't date a stand-up comic.

And whatever you do, don't get with someone who is only 50 percent of what you want. You'll end up either reminding him of that everyday or spending most of your time strategizing about how to turn him into something he is not. If you love tall men, don't wake up every morning measuring your boyfriend, saying, "Damn! You still five foot seven!"

Regardless of what you think you are looking for in a

life partner, the truth is, you can't predict who you'll fall in love with. Love can occur out of nowhere. A man and a woman who have been platonic friends for years can fall in love with each other after sharing one unplanned and unexpected kiss. Then *boom*! Just like that, they see each other totally differently.

No one can explain why black women always say, "He gotta be at least six feet tall," yet a lot of short brothas I know are happily married. That means somebody out there loves the short man!

Why do people attempt long-distance relationships, despite the fact that they are difficult to sustain? How come a woman will leave her home at any hour of the night when the right man calls and tells her to come over? (Well, actually, we know what that's about.) The point is, since the beginning of time, love has always been the mighty X factor. It's not always rational, and it doesn't really make sense. I have witnessed women with MBAs settling down with men who only have their high school diplomas, and I am sure those women didn't go into graduate school saying, "I can't wait to marry a man at the top of his GED night school class!"

With this in mind, rather than viewing your list as the be-all and end-all where finding a mate is concerned, consider it a blueprint that's subject to revisions. You'll never find a man with exactly everything you desire, no matter how reasonable and sensible your list may seem. Think about it. Do you really want to be a lonely, seventy-year-old woman, still tied to a list and adding things like, ". . . and he has to have his own teeth"?

Determine what you absolutely must have in a man in order to be consistently happy. When you find a guy that has most of what you are looking for, learn to compromise and love him for who he is. After all, he might be compromising some of the things he wanted when he decided to settle down with you. No one is perfect. The key to longevity with someone is realizing early on that working together with your near-perfect man can lead both of you to a perfect union.

CHAPTER THREE
the approach

Bedtime stories promise gallant knights, risking their lives to save damsels in distress. Well, it's been a while since I've seen a real knight or even a horse, and these days if you call a woman a damsel, she might slap you. In fact, today's knights are likely to run a woman over with their horse if she doesn't give up the digits in a timely manner.

Times have definitely changed.

Back in the old days, a man would approach a woman he didn't know, extend his hand, and introduce himself. The woman would then politely shake his hand, introduce herself, and say, "Nice to meet you." Today, if a man sees a woman he would like to get to know, instead of walking over to her, he simply would shout from wherever he is standing:

"Aye, Shawty, what yo' name is? You look good in dem jeans! Any room for me? I know you heard me! Don't make

me chase you! Why it gotta be like that? Why you walking faster! Well, walk on then, you ain't all that! You need to fix your attitude! My girl looks way better than you, anyway!"

Proper introductions have become so rare that when a guy *is* extremely well mannered, charming, funny, complimentary, and original with his approach, women immediately put their guard up or run the other way. Take this conversation I recently overheard between two sistas:

"I met this fantastic guy at Super Wal-Mart today, girl. He was cute, he was tall; nice and funny. He walked me to my car and helped me put my groceries and new DVD rack in the trunk. But something just didn't seem right about old boy, so I sucker punched him, jumped in the car, and took off. He could have been a serial killer, saying stuff like, "You look very beautiful today." It's the nice ones that have a basement full of dead bodies, you know. That reminds me, *CSI: Miami* comes on tonight."

Pick-up Lines

Know this: When men approach women with stupid, corny lines, they are saying, "I know I have no shot at you, but I am not letting you walk by me without saying something." They are actually trying to give you a compliment. And you're probably thinking, *Why don't men just say hello?*

Duh! That's too simple. We only think to say that if our clever pick-up line doesn't work. In fact, as soon as you say you are not interested and walk away, that's when we say, "Damn, I should have just said hello."

Some men think that pick-up lines are harmless fun and women should just have a sense of humor. Other men say they do it because they want to get a reaction out of the woman. It doesn't matter if the reaction is good or bad, just as long as she notices them. For example, old men's pick-up lines usually start with, "If I was just a few years younger . . ." Disrespectful old men's pick-up lines are similar, but the word "Viagra" is usually somewhere up in the mix. And men that are old, but who still think they got it going on, always offer to pay for something when they say hello. "Hey, Ms. Lady. If you ever need your rent paid or help with your car note or want me to buy you a new Honda Accord, let Rufus know. Those young guys don't know how to take care of something like you."

What *is* a great pick-up line? A great pick-up line for a man is anything we can come up with to get a woman we don't know to smile and stick around long enough until we ultimately say something stupid or repeat a question she's already answered, like, "So who are you here with? Oh, that's right, you did say. My bad."

I don't use them, but I like to hear pick-up lines, especially if they are funny. Here are some of my favorites:

- Your legs must be tired, because you've been running through my mind all day.
- One in four black men are incarcerated, guy number two is gay, and guy number three has two baby mommas. Now that leaves me—so what you gonna do?
- Did it hurt when you fell from heaven?
- I lost my phone number. Can I have yours?
- Your father must be a mason, because he built a brick house!
- Excuse me, miss, did you fart? Because you just blew me away!
- Are you wearing space pants? Because your ass is out of this world!
- Were you arrested earlier? It's got to be illegal to look that good!
- I hope you know CPR, because you take my breath away.
- Do you take karate? Because your body's kickin'!
- You must wash your pants with Windex, because I can see myself in them.
- Your body is like a temple; it needs to be worshipped.

Yes, many of these lines are corny, but don't lie. Some of them got you smiling, and if any of them is uttered by the right guy at the right time, you'll either pretend you didn't hear it (you're in denial that he's so lame) or give a fake giggle and play with your hair as though you just got the best compliment ever.

The Lesson to Be Learned from Jeromeo ......

Women, picture this: You are in a club, having a good time with your girlfriends. All of a sudden, out of nowhere, a guy walks right up to you and flashes his I-know-you-want-me smile. You look him up and down and bust out laughing. Why are you laughing, knowing it's never cool to be rude? Because this dude in his two-piece red suit has a very drippy Jheri curl that could be a fire hazard if the deejay started playing reggae music and people waved their lighters. To your horror, he also has four gold teeth that he is actually polishing in front of you with a cocktail napkin. And he is so blinged out, but with the fakest jewelry known to the twenty-five-cent gumball machine.

Now what makes this guy approach you, or anybody else for that matter, besides confidence? How about the fact that whether you tell "Jeromeo" you would love to dance with him and then have his children, or flat out laugh in his face and tell him to beat it, he knows the worst thing you can say is no—a couple of times. He gets rejected or told no all the time. In fact, he probably expects it and wipes that rejection off his shoulders, along with the excess activator juice. Nonetheless, Jeromeo is still there to have a good time, and knowing him, he will ask you to introduce him to one of your girlfriends who came to party, because *you* are taking up space and wasting his time.

The majority of people, especially women who are not as bold and persistent as Jeromeo, could learn one thing from him: There is nothing wrong with approaching and attempting to meet someone new! Single women should do it more often. The number of cool guys you'll actually meet, as opposed to the *zero* that you are meeting right now, would surprise you.

Girl, It's Your Turn ······························

Elderly churchgoing women love to tell single young women to be patient and wait. God will send you the man you seek. That may be true, but God also helps those who help themselves. You think Eve waited when she wanted an apple? Okay, bad analogy, but you get what I am saying.

Black women have made so many strides in business, medicine, academics, and politics. For you to bite your acrylic nails when it comes to approaching men would make black female pioneers turn over in their graves. If Harriet Tubman could approach black men and ask them to run away to freedom (". . . and by the way, if weez get caught, master will kill us dead!") you can ask a man to the movies.

Now does this mean you walk up and down the mall wearing one of those double-sided wooden sandwich boards, advertising that you are open for mingling with a 20 percent off coupon? Of course not. But actively putting yourself in a position to meet new people is a start.

Now, I understand that there are some women who will think that I just asked them to donate a kidney. You might be either too shy or too set in your ways, or you've simply told yourself that approaching a man first is not something you want to do. I know, I know. What if he is involved with some-one already? What if he thinks you are desperate, or worse, what if he is simply not interested? (Like any of those things will kill you, right?) Some women think approaching a man is a big deal, but I want to tell you right now, it isn't. Men like it!

Just to relieve some of your apprehension, I'll let you in on a little secret: You are absolutely wrong if you think we want to talk all night long to the guy we came with. We already know that fool. We want to get to know *you*. If I'm lying, I'm dying.

Here are some other things to consider that might ease your jitters:

- Men will never be as hard on you as women are on us when we try to meet you.
- Men will not suck their teeth and pretend to have asthma if you tap us on the shoulder to say hello.
- Men absolutely will not think you are desperate, easy, or crazy if you approach us first. Remember, we are the ones who are desperate, easy, and crazy.

IS THERE LOVE AT THE CLUB? ···············

Is the club an ideal place to find Mr. Right? In my opinion, no. Clubs are loud, people are drunk, no one is honest, you hardly ever connect with people you meet, and everyone is text messaging other people that are not in the club. Plus, everyone is into the *group thing,* meaning we come in groups, we dance in groups, and women still go to the bathroom in groups. Add obnoxious men spoiling the mood of a woman a good guy wants to talk to, and bitter, man-hating women blocking their girlfriends from talking to guys they wouldn't mind meeting. Oh, and I almost forgot, it's dark. You often have to walk outside to get a good look at who you have been talking to all night. "That's a mighty big Adam's apple you have there, Veronica. I didn't notice that when we were inside."

When You See Him but He Doesn't Notice You, What to *Do*?

Dear single ladies,

I am writing this letter to inform you that when you see a guy you want to get to know, but he is not giving you any eye contact or conversation, all is not lost. Just follow these four easy steps:

Step 1: Get close enough that he notices your presence.
Step 2: Smile at him, but look away and shake your head, like he reminds you of an old friend or a good memory. He should definitely be curious about why you are so happy, and more important, he's wondering if he has anything to do with that good thought in your head. Now be sure to look away, because the

whole thing has to be natural. If you stare at him too long, just smiling, he will think you are crazy (especially if you live in New York City and you're on a subway train).

Step 3: If he does not comment or inquire about what has you in a good mood or why you are smiling at him, play it cool and walk away. If he's not interested in your thoughts, then you can rule him out immediately and move on. Remember, the ultimate goal is to find a man who cares about you and what you are thinking. If he does show interest, proceed to the next step.

Step 4: If he asks what's so funny, answer one of two ways:

1) Be honest. Introduce yourself and tell him you find him attractive. This will no doubt catch him off guard, make him smile back, and gets right to the point. Is this superbold and aggressive on your part? Hell, yes! Only certain type of women can pull this off or even feel comfortable being so direct. But you will find out right then and there if he has any interest in you and what his current relationship situation is.

2) Make up a story. That's right, be a little dishonest. Okay, actually just tell him a lie. Men tell women lies all the time, so don't feel guilty. A little lie won't hurt anyone. It won't make you a bad person. Plus, you don't know the dude. It's not like you lied to a friend. Now that we've gotten the moral issue out of the way, tell him that he reminds you of a good friend from high school who all the girls liked; who stayed in trouble so much, he was always in detention. Believe it or not,

most men will actually find that very flattering. "So let me see if I understand this right. I remind you of a cute, bad boy from your high school who all the girls liked, huh? Girl, you better give me your number, so we can have some babies!" (Did you notice how he threw in "cute"?) Seriously, after you've said something like that and he realizes that the reason you are staring and smiling has nothing to do with him having spinach in his teeth or toilet paper stuck to his shoe, he will inquire more about you and this "bad boy" he reminds you of, just to keep the conversation going.

So let's reel in this fish. If he responds well to either the lie or the truth, and seems interested, pull back on your fishing line and listen to see if he can carry a conversation and is worth planning a phone date, and then possibly a real date. Red Lobster, here you come! Good luck!

Sincerely,

Finesse

When approaching a guy, be natural, be confident, and have fun with it. What's the worse thing that can happen? Absolutely nothing. The same nothing that may be going on in your social life right now. So take a chance!

And to be honest, almost all brothas are approachable—even the one chillin' in the corner. You see, chillin' is low stress. We get to stare at women all night, we don't have to split our drink money in half, and we can play out any type conversation with you in our heads to blasting music, which actually gives our imaginations a soundtrack. If you see men doing that, we are perfect targets and open for any conversation. Walking over and just chillin' with a guy is a great way to meet somebody new. Eventually you two will notice the same things, laugh at the same jokes, and pick out the worst- and best-dressed people together. Before you know it, the both of you will be talking up a storm.

Approaching a guy first is actually a no-lose situation, because if he is not interested, he'll still smile, thank you for the compliment, and keep it moving (freeing you to move on to the next guy). Or the conversation will immediately let you know you are in the possible "cool-friend" zone, and you can parlay this into meeting new people in his world, thereby broadening your social circle. You may learn about events, bars, lounges, house parties, etc., you didn't even know existed.

If absolutely nothing comes of your attempt to be proactive, and he doesn't catch the hint or appreciate the effort you made to say something to him, he's not for you—no matter how attractive or intriguing he looked from across the room. Make a smooth exit and keep it moving. Pick another guy, another time. Just know that you did not play yourself or come off as desperate. Remember, your goal is to have a man respond in a way that shows he gives a damn.

With that being said, since I am letting you know men are easy targets 85 percent of the time, do us a favor: If you know you are desperate, easy, or crazy, simply give us a hint as to which one you happen to be before it's too late. It's only fair. Desperate is something we can get to the bottom of together. Easy is not necessarily a bad thing unless the mobile clinic makes weekly stops at your house to restock your medicine cabinet. But crazy is not welcome under any circumstances. Fix crazy first, and then come holla! Men will only drive an unstable woman crazier.

Mission Impossible: Figuring Guys Out ········

It would be easy if every guy you met had his real intentions stamped on his forehead. Then you could just read to find out which guy was right for you. Imagine the drama you could avoid just by looking. You'd have guys all figured out! Here's what the warning signs could be like:

- I WANT TO HAVE SEX WITH YOU, AND THEN MOVE ON TO SOMEONE ELSE.
- I WANT TO HAVE SEX WITH YOU, AND THEN MOVE IN, BECAUSE I NEED A PLACE TO STAY.
- I WANT TO HAVE SEX WITH YOU AND LET YOU CHAUFFEUR ME AROUND, BECAUSE I HAVE NO CAR.
- I WANT TO HAVE SEX WITH YOU AND ASK ABOUT YOUR NEXT PAYDAY, BECAUSE I ALWAYS NEED A LOAN.
- I WANT TO HAVE SEX WITH YOU, BUT I WILL ALWAYS BE ON MY CELL PHONE OR TEXT MESSAGING SOMEONE ELSE EVERY MINUTE OF THE DAY. I DISAPPEAR A LOT, AND RIGHT WHEN YOU'RE ABOUT TO WRITE ME OFF, I'LL POP BACK UP WITH EXPLANATIONS THAT MAKE SENSE ONLY TO ME.

- I AM SUPERNICE, LOVE TO SHOP, BUT AM TOO SOFT SPOKEN AND NEVER BRING UP HAVING SEX WITH YOU, EVER.
- I WANT TO HAVE SEX WITH YOU AND FINANCIALLY TAKE CARE OF YOU FOR THE REST OF YOUR LIFE. BUT IF I EVER CATCH YOU LOOKING AT ANOTHER GUY LONGER THAN THREE SECONDS, I WILL GIVE YOU A BLACK EYE.
- I WANT TO HAVE SEX WITH YOU . . . AND EVERY OTHER GIRL THAT WANTS TO HAVE SEX WITH ME. BUT YOU ARE MY "MAIN GIRL" AND THUS DIFFERENT FROM THE REST.
- I WANT TO HAVE SEX WITH YOU AND AM A NICE GUY. BUT MY EX-GIRLFRIEND IS STANDING RIGHT BEHIND ME, BREATHING HARD, WITH A BRICK IN HER HAND, STARING AT YOU, LIKE "GIRL, I WISH YOU WOULD!"
- I WANT TO HAVE SEX WITH YOU AND AM THE MOST HANDSOME GUY TO EVER HAVE AN INTEREST IN YOU. BUT I HAVE SO MANY KIDS FROM DIFFERENT WOMEN, YOU FEEL PREGNANT JUST READING MY FOREHEAD.

In real life, these guys are all in the dating game, but there is no warning on their foreheads. Unfortunately you have to figure out who's who and what's what. They have no specific age, no specific size, and their skin color has no specific shade of brown. These brothas are confident and comfortable with who they are and their current situation.

THEIR MISSION: to get you comfortable with who they are and their current situation.

THEIR BIGGEST WEAPON: your eagerness to get involved with someone. They hope that your desire to *not* be alone and have someone show you some kind of attention and affection will help you totally overlook their pretty obvious shortcomings. [Note: Shortcomings may include not being gainfully employed, lacking valid ID, or using check-cashing centers as a primary means of banking.] These types of guys will all claim to be on the come up and say, "With the right girl by my side, the sky is the limit." Don't believe it.

THIS BOOK WILL SELF-DESTRUCT IF YOU TELL ANYONE I TOLD YOU THAT. SHHH!

THE TOP FIVE WAYS TO MAKE A FIRST MOVE ON A GUY

1) Flirt! Your eyes are magic.
When a woman purposely makes continuous eye contact with a man she doesn't know, he will instantly be intrigued, and his eye contact in return won't be so subtle. If he is interested, he will stare back even if it's just to make sure he is reading your glances correctly. He doesn't want to mistake flirty eye conversation for what it's not. He has to make sure you are saying, "Hi, sexy, come get to know me." And not, "Hey, fool, don't you owe me money?" If he never returns your come-hither eye invitation, he is not interested, and you never had to actually approach him.

2) Flirt more! Give your prospect a big smile.

There is so much power in a smile. It says, "I am happy. Come share some of this happiness with me, big daddy." Giving a man the impression that every time he looks your way, you can't help but blush, is inviting and easy to read. A man who is interested will definitely come and see what all the high-cheekbone action is about.

3) Be direct.

Just give him a compliment about anything. We love to know we have admirable qualities. Even the toughest thug is weak when it comes to a positive comment from a woman. "Girl, you better stop talking all that truth." Do not use pick-up lines, though! Pick-up lines don't work for us, and we won't take you seriously if you sound too rehearsed or say something corny. Just keep it simple, because men are simple. "You smell nice" works. Now when I think about it, I don't know if you can technically smell *nice*, but it sounds good and we love to hear it.

4) Send a friend over with a simple message.

If you can't do it, send a friend to do all the work. "My friend thinks you're cute." No more, no less. Nothing else needs to be said.

5) Buy him a drink.

If you are in a club, before you even ask his name, simply say, "So, what are you drinking?" A real pimp move is to find out what he's drinking on your own and hand him a fresh one or send the waitress over with one when his drink gets low. If he does not come over to say thank you, walk over and tell him how much he owes you for the drink. I'm serious.

The Female Mack Daddy! ·

"The first thing she ever said to me was, 'Okay, so all I'm gonna say is, smell like that one mo' time and I'm gonna have to make you my boyfriend.' Then she ran her fingers across my chest as she walked away. I was hooked, dawg! I followed her to the bar, and I have been following ever since."

—Ryan, actor, twenty-nine, Hollywood

There are women out there who take matters into their own hands. When these women see a guy they like, and the opportunity permits, they don't wait to be approached by him. They make the first move. Whether it's a compliment followed by an inviting smile, or an aggressive full-court press flirtation, they don't leave anything to chance. They straight up let a brotha know they are interested, and in all honesty, I like this type of woman a lot!

Being more proactive when it comes to meeting men is a good thing. We welcome that approach with open arms. In fact, I think we voted yes to that at the first Million Man

March. I mean, let's face it, the good old days when a man would not only approach you like royalty but would take off his coat and lay it across a puddle for you to walk over are long gone. Remember when men did that? Me neither, but some dumb ass must have done that a long time ago for people to still make reference to it today.

HE/SHE MUST BE GAY

Here's a question: Why do black people automatically think the person we tried to pick up is gay if we get shot down? Men say a woman is gay if she never gives us a chance and never goes anywhere without her girlfriends. Women say a man is gay if he is "too attractive" or "pretty" and if the man is not interested. Here are two examples of what I mean:

Scenario #1: Black Man Picking up a Black Woman at a Restaurant
BM: Excuse me, um . . . Hi, what's up? I'm Eric. What's your name?
BW: (*deep breath*) Stacy.
BM: I hope I am not bothering you, but I saw you sitting over here, alone, looking all sad, wearing black, like you just came from a funeral or something. (*He chuckles.*)

BW: I did.

BM: Oh, my bad. Well, I hope you feel better. (*He points to his boys a couple of tables away. They each do their own individual corny acknowledgment. One guy tips a fake hat. Another shoots a fake gun at her.*) Me and my friends over there was just saying that you are too beautiful to be sitting alone, looking all sad, so I thought I'd come over and invite you to—

BW: Look . . . um, what's your name again? Ernest?

BM: Eric. It's Eric.

BW: Look, Eric, now is not a good time for me. I just want to be left alone.

BM: Okay, I understand. Who died?

BW: None of your business. Could you please just leave?

BM: Okay, my bad. Calm down. I was just trying to come over and spread a little sunshine.

BW: Good-bye, Ernie!

BM: All right, all right. I can tell you don't want to be bothered. I hope you feel better.

BW: Thanks.

BM: It's Eric, by the way.

BW: Excuse me?

BM: You said Ernie or something.

BW: (*quick fake smile*)

BM: Well, if you ever want to—

BW: I don't.

BM: Cool, cool. Well, I'll go now. I hope you feel better.

BW: (*silence*)

Eric goes back over and sits at his table. His boys are anxious.

BM FRIEND #1: So, what happened, dawg?

BM: She's gay.

Scenario #2: Black Woman Picking up a Black Man at a Club

BW: Hey, sexy.

BM: (*smiling*) Hey, what's up?

BW: (*sniffing and leaning into his personal space*) Damn, you smell good.

BM: Thank you.

BW: (*takes sips of her vodka cranberry*) You wanna dance?

BM: No thanks.

BW: Awww, it's like that?

BM: I just came to chill. I have a girlfriend.

BW: Good for you. Well, tell her I said she can't be leaving you alone like that. Somebody's going to kidnap you! (*Big laugh as she takes another sip.*)

BM: (*light laughter*) Okay, I'll tell her.

BW: Bye, sexy.

BM: Be safe.

BW: Hey, all right now. You better stop that.

BM: (*confused*) Stop what?

BW: You so cute. (*She smells him again and smoothly runs her hand across his chest as she walks off. She walks over to her girlfriends by the bar.*)

BW FRIEND #1: Girl, who was that?!

BW: I don't know. Some dude.

> BW GIRLFRIEND #2: He was cute. Did you get his
> number?
> BW: No, he said he had a girl, but you know what that
> means.
> ALL: He's gay.

Am I making something out of nothing, or are you guilty of this too?

Why He Might Not Be Approaching You · · · · · · ·

I know a lot of good guys who have approached women at social functions and were rejected in a not-so-pleasant way. They've passed that bad experience along to their friends, and their friends shared it with *their* friends. And you know the story changed along the way. "Remember Mike? He was at the bar the other night, and he asked this girl what her name was and she threw battery acid on his face! These women be trippin', son! Be careful!"

Now, guys don't bother approaching women the old way. Our new philosophy is if you came to have a good time with your girls, we came to chill out with our boys. Do we want to meet you? Yes. Possibly have drinks with you and dance with you? Yes. Will we approach you and tell you that? Probably not. It's like men had a private meeting and we decided that we are no longer encountering women we don't know on a whim. It could be that men are tired of approaching women who act single by letting us buy them drinks and grinding on our jeans all night long, only to claim to be seriously involved with someone when we ask for their number. Or men could be tired of dealing with the fear of rejection and embarrassment.

Since we can never predict how some women will respond to our advances, there are an increasing number of guys who opt to chill and watch the show from the sidelines. Experience has taught them that it's better to enjoy the night alone than have some woman make them feel bad for trying to be friendly. That's all we want to do, no matter how rude or unintelligent we might come across when we search our brain for those perfect words that will unlock your heart, like, "I want to get you pregnant. How's Thursday work for you?"

I've talked to a lot of guys who say that you can approach black women on a real humble tip, and they still get an instant attitude or, even worse, they ignore you. How cold is that when a woman pretends like she didn't even hear you? "Well, excuse me for bothering you! I was confused when I saw you in a night club, because that usually means you want to be around loud music and people who are here to party. My bad. I'll go ask the deejay to turn the music down and also bring you some warm milk and a good book to read."

Now is a perfect time for me to talk about the Mean Chick. Men often don't approach these women because they look, well, unapproachable. I know women hear that all the time, but the truth is the truth. It may not be you, but you know you have a girlfriend that looks like she punches brick walls for a living.

No matter where you guys hang out, she is complaining or angry about something. "This club is whack, these dudes are whack, this music is whack," and that would be cool and understandable if you were actually *at* the club. But you both are still in the mirror doing your hair. You haven't even left the house yet, and she is screaming the world is whack. And when you finally get to the club, she wonders why people walk up to her saying folks are smoking weed in the VIP section or that two girls are fighting in the bathroom. It's because your girlfriend, usually dressed in all black, stands in one place the entire night looking stern with her arms folded across her chest. Folks have confused her for *club security*.

Do you have a girlfriend like that? No? You might be her, then, because every girl knows someone like that. All too often I see single women stand around in social settings and look like they are number 398 on the DMV line, which is now serving number 16. That's why men who do take a shot at actually saying hello to you always start off by saying, "Why are you looking so mean?" Or "Smile!" Don't you hate it when we say that? Well, stop looking so mean! Fix your face, nod your head to the beat, wiggle your hips, show at least one tooth, unfold your arms, and wave your hands in the air like you just don't care—and stop looking like the last person picked for kickball.

Mr. Stare-a-Lot

Have you ever had a guy stare at you all night, but never bother to approach you? Then when you are about to leave the club, he waves to you or motions for you to come over to him? That's whack, right? Here's what guys who do that are thinking:

1) If you are going to turn him down, it might as well be at the end of the night, so he doesn't ruin his whole evening at the club thinking about how he struck out with you.
2) He'd rather wait it out and see if he has a chance with you than talk to anyone else that is a distant second or third choice.
3) He's not pressed to meet anyone at all, which is a good thing, because most guys try and talk to anything with breasts. So Mr. Stare-a-Lot would rather listen to good music and stare at your fine ass all night long. Or it could be that you look familiar and he is trying to figure out if he owes you money.
4) He thinks he's playing it cool and giving you space to party with whomever you are there with. If you are with your girls, he'll chill and try to wave you over when you get tired of the all-girl dance circle.

Now, if you have no intentions of ever talking to Mr. Stare-a-Lot, *do not* stare back at him or look in his direction more than twice. We take this type of eye contact as code for "I want to know you and possibly have your baby." He will think you are interested, and he will strike up a conversation before the night is over.

IT MIGHT SOUND CRAZY, BUT . . .

Men will watch a woman all night, but never get the nerve to go over and say anything. The minute somebody else goes over and talks to you, and you respond favorably, like you have been waiting for someone to come over, in our head we are cussing you out for cheating on us in front of our faces. "How is she going to talk to him right in front of me? After all we've been through. Get away from my girlfriend, fool! I was about to tell her we go together before you walked over there!"

Men are looking for a sign from you that it is okay for them to approach. If we don't see any indication that you would like to meet us, we think random "man thoughts," like:

· *She got a man.*
· *She waiting to turn somebody down and make them feel stupid.*
· *As soon as I say hello, she is going to make a screeching-teeth-suck sound loud enough for the bouncers standing outside the club to hear.*

> · *She is pregnant.*
> · *As soon as I walk over to her, a man will drop from the ceiling, screaming, "Get away from my girl!"*

Three Is Not a Crowd ··························

Third-party introductions, made by a male or female friend, are absolutely the best and easiest way to meet someone new. Here's why: someone else is doing all of the initial talking and, whether they realize it or not, vouching for you. Moreover, these types of meet-and-greets can occur just about anywhere—at a party, in church, or even over a coffee at Starbucks. It could go something like this: "Tony, this is my friend Jackie. She teaches at Douglass High School and went to Clark Atlanta. Jackie, this is my boy Tony. Tony barely graduated from Morehouse, but somehow, he became the principal of Beecher Hills Elementary School."

Just like that, two people have something to talk about, and no one feels any pressure to be clever. Now whatever happens next is up to Jackie and Tony. People are always more open to seeing what someone is about if they were referred to them by a friend. Even in business, it's easier and more comforting to do business with someone a good friend knows rather than a complete stranger. Now, I didn't say it was *better*, because a lot of people have horror stories about doing business with friends and friends of friends. But there is an initial comfort factor knowing a friend's friend recommended someone to you. Let's weigh in.

PROS
- You don't have to do all the talking, and introductions almost always go smoothly.
- Even if you don't make a love connection, you meet someone new and maybe start a great friendship that could lead you to other new people.

CONS
- The person who introduced you may like you too, and only wanted you to meet his friends. He or she had no intentions of you two liking each other or having an instant love connection. And now you've come between two friends.
- The person ends up being sooo obnoxious that it causes you to have second thoughts about the judgment—and state of mind—of the friend who made the introduction.

Most of the women I have dated were actually introduced to me by a mutual friend. The hard part comes when you have to be interesting enough to keep the conversation going when the mutual friend walks away. So there is still work to be done. Being witty, charismatic, and funny always helps a man in any conversation with a woman. But women should also make an effort too. Even if you have no interest whatsoever in the person you were introduced to, it's always good to be nice. Guys tell other guys all the time, "Oh, I met Tanya. She's cool as hell." And trust me, they take note.

I once took my good friend, named NYC, to a sports bar in Atlanta, because she wanted to get out of the house. I told her I was going to watch the Atlanta Falcons football game, and she said that was her favorite team and asked if she could tag along. I didn't mind the company since I was rolling solo. When I picked her up, she came out of the house wearing a rather nice, come-get-me outfit, which made me instantly but very tactfully inquire about her intentions. So trying not to make her feel uncomfortable, I said something, like, "What in the hell are you wearing? You trying to watch a game or run some game?"

When we got there, the place was packed. It also didn't take long for me to figure out that my friend knew nothing about the Falcons or football. When women say things, like, "How can you see if the players are cute if they wear masks all the time," you know they know nothing about sports. So as I explained the game to her, we drank, we ate, and she mingled.

NYC was meeting some cool guys as my team was losing (again). When I was ready to leave, she saw one she thought was cute and asked me to go over and do the introductions, since I had been watching the game the whole time and not helping her meet men. Go figure (right?). Normally I would have done it, but I was in a bad mood since my team lost, again. Plus, I thought NYC should just walk up to the guy and simply say hello and see what happens. I told NYC that she had to get over the fear of making the first move. I gave her my best Denzel Washington, *Remember the Titans/Malcolm X* speech. "We didn't land on Plymouth Rock, Plymouth Rock landed on us! Now go out there and win!"

She eventually worked up the nerve to go over there. . . . When she came back after talking with the guy, she was pregnant. Just kidding! She said she was scared as hell when she was walking over to him, but as soon as she got close and was about to say hello, he told her that she looked very familiar and the conversation just flowed from there. She said that he was cool, but he was currently in a relationship. He invited her to a party later on that night, one she had being trying to get an invitation to all week.

Later, NYC went to the party with one of her girlfriends. She saw the guy again, and he introduced her to his girlfriend and more of his friends. She later told me she had a blast that night. She had met some cool women, which is hard to do nowadays, and some cute guys that thought she was cool as hell.

WHEN POSSIBLE HAVE A MALE FRIEND DO YOUR DIRTY WORK ·

It's better for a guy to tell another guy that you are interested versus having your girlfriend do it. Your male friends, at most times, have your best interest at heart and won't mess up the message. "My girl Sharon likes you." The man receiving the message won't ever respond by saying something, like, "That's cool, but what about me and you?" If that is the case, you obviously didn't have a chance from the start. But when a woman is the go-between and the man responds by saying, "That's cool, but I actually had my eye on you for a long time." Aw hell . . . No matter how delicately this situation is handled, it will never have a good outcome.

The Bottom Line

So let's recap. You are going to have to make an effort to go out and meet people. And you are going to have to either: 1) approach a guy, 2) look like you are receptive to guys approaching you, or 3) have a friend start talking you up like you're an Amway product.

CHAPTER FOUR
the dating game

Back in grade school, getting a girlfriend or boyfriend was as easy as passing a note in class. You remember the note, don't you?

Do you like me?
Check ❑ yes ❑ no or ❑ maybe so.

If you checked yes, you had a girlfriend or boyfriend for a week until you two started fighting over the red crayon, and you decided it was not going to work. Around middle school, guys and girls stopped sending those types of notes, because girls would just straight up tell boys that they liked them, and then they'd be a couple. Since we had a lot of cute girls at my school, it always worked out for the boys (the more things change, the more they stay the same). Then every month or so, people would break up and date one another's best friend. Ah, the good old days.

In high school, boys did most of the pursuing, 'cause our hormones were raging, and y'all started looking like women overnight. In college it was a free-for-all. College is a young folks' home where every possible scenario for people hooking up, dating, hating, one-night stands, engagements, betrayals, and happy endings gets played out on a semester or quarterly basis (and that's only the action that goes on when you're still sober).

You'd think that when we finally grew up, graduated from school, and started real jobs, we'd stop playing games . . . but that is when the dating game *really* begins.

The Game of Dating ···························

Now, some people hate the fact that dating is considered a game. They think that it makes a joke out of something that should be serious. After all, if more people took dating seriously, we probably wouldn't have so many crazy people walking around, bitter and evil. Relationships (even short ones) help define who you become as a person. That is very serious business! And anyone who has ever had his or her heart broken will tell you that there is nothing playful about dating.

But I've gotta tell you, I've always looked at it as a game and here's why: First, it's hard to figure out who is being truthful and who is just playing around. For example, he might say, "How do I know your real name is Kim?" and she might ask, "How do I know you are really an astronaut?"

Second, some people strategically plot and plan how to get next to the one they like, and then pretend it was "fate" or "chance" that brought them together. He's been clocking your Laundromat routine for months, unbeknownst to you. Then one day, when you're about to load the dryer, he pops out from nowhere with "Care for a Bounce dryer sheet?"

Others jump online, pointing and clicking to the one they like, but then describe themselves as a ten when they really are an eight. How do you know what number you really are? Go look in a mirror and shout out the number that comes to you, then subtract two.

Dating is an investment. For women, it could be the money spent on hair, nails, makeup, fragrances, and clothes. For us men, it's what we spend on grooming, cars, personal fitness, and other stuff that we think y'all like. The more disposable income men have, the more we can invest into whatever we think you'd enjoy.

For example, men like houses. But men also know that women *really* like houses. If women preferred two-bedroom apartments than big houses, eight out of ten men would live in two-bedroom apartments and never think twice about yard work again. Money can attract and lack of it definitely repels. In my experience, black women don't like broke men—plain and simple. If a brother has a bad year, a good sister will stick by him, but by the 366th day his ass is officially single, without her ever having to announce her departure.

The majority of men know the majority of women like money very, very much. And don't be offended by me saying that women are attracted to money either. Remember, this book is about what men think, and every man knows that women are ultimately attracted to security and stability! No woman likes moving twice a year. No woman likes having her phone temporarily disconnected all the time. No woman likes hearing gunshots and stray cats outside of her window every night. And although candlelit meals can be romantic, no woman likes getting dressed by candlelight, brushing her teeth by candlelight, reading a book in bed by candlelight, and investigating a noise they heard in their two-bedroom apartment by candlelight. Seriously, I don't know one woman, especially a black woman, who likes to struggle.

Sizing Him Up

You can tell a lot about a man by his shoes. Every woman I know thinks the size of a man's shoe is an indication of the size of his genitalia, but I'm here to tell you a lot of guys are hip to that, so they purposely wear size twelve shoes when they are actually a seven. By the time you figured that out, you'll already be four months into the relationship, and you both will be sitting around wondering why the toilet paper goes so quickly in the house—you were padding your bra, and he was stuffing his shoes.

If you have never bought into the size-of-a-man's-feet

thing, good for you. The *condition* a man's shoes are in, however, is very important. If he is wearing his Sunday's best, and you can see the meat on his feet and he ain't wearing sandals, he might be abusive. It takes a certain level of I-don't-give-a-damn to wear out a pair of shoes to the point where your feet are on display. It's one thing to have holes in your socks, but holes in your kicks? That's ridiculous. Nice shoes mean a brother takes pride in his appearance.

You can tell a lot about a man without him saying a word. Rough hands, dirty nails, and ashy knuckles mean one of two things: either this man works hard for a living or has just done hard time in prison. Soft hands or manicured hands mean a brother works more with his mind than with his hands, or he loves the hell out of himself when he is alone and always keeps a steady supply of moisturizer around for those intimate moments.

When a brother owns a nice, clean car, it says a lot about his maintenance of everything he holds dear in his life. It may even reflect a brother's success in business or his financial status. But watch out—it could also mean he is horrible with prioritizing and the fool bought a Mercedes, but still lives with his mother. Here's a tip: If a man has a nice expensive car, but he always wants to go to your place at the end of a date, he more than likely lives with his woman, his mother, or he actually lives in that car. Back in my struggling comic days, I used to tell women I take care of my mom, so she lives with me. But my mom was the only one working, all the bills were in her name, and I still slept in the same bed I use to wet when I was six years old. When my brother moved out, I just pushed the two twin beds together and bought king-size sheets and a comforter.

But please know you can absolutely never judge a book *only* by its cover. Today, wealthy men dress like teenagers. Serial killers dress like businessmen. Religious men dress in golf shirts and slacks and carry man purses full of pamphlets that tell you how to improve the world by starting with yourself. So take the time to really get to know a man beyond any superficial bells and whistles that peak your curiosity.

The Playing Field ·····························

Since women outnumber men in the black community, and since the media loves to bring up the fact that one in ten black men (or some other depressing number like that) in my age group are in jail, we free men understand, for black women, dating is getting really competitive. The numbers don't lie. There are more of you than us, and we know it. If you want a man who is responsible, reliable, respectful, dependable, hardworking, trustworthy (they do exist), gainfully employed (it can happen), not already married (it's not a myth), wants to get married in a time frame that you can deal with, and will share that magic number of desired kids (dream big), realize that competition is fierce. You've got to be aware of the other players in the game.

YOUNGSTERS

Younger females are coming into the "adults only" dating game without any of the old-school inhibitions. I don't condone grown men approaching and dating teenagers, but the reality is that it happens all the time. Underage women are not waiting until they are twenty-one to flood the nightclubs and get their party on. Whether they have fake IDs or just plain "know somebody," they are constantly around grown men, acting "grown." The sad part is that men used to say, "You're how old? Oh, you're jailbait, get away from me." But these days, not every man is saying that, and these youngsters are wearing way too much lip gloss and screaming, "Shake what ya momma gave ya!" on the dance floor. Now whether they get the results they want or learn hard lessons the hard way, they are always trying to be noticed.

Younger guys are also in the game. The young guns out there shooting up the town (sometimes literally) have an entirely different playbook than the thirty-plus guys. They are anxious, eager, and superexcited to be around women in general. More and more older women are hooking up with younger guys (which seems to be more socially acceptable now, unless she is his PE teacher). He wants an experienced woman, because he thinks the women his age are not on "his level." She is looking for a man with some energy, and young Aaron is cute and came knocking first. It all fits together nicely. He approached her first. She called him a baby and threatened to spank him if he didn't run along. He said, "You know you want to get your groove back, Ms. Stella." She asked her girlfriends' opinions. They said, "Why the hell not? If you won't, I will," and then made some kind of Similac joke. Later that week Ms. Stella invited the young buck over to watch *The Matrix* on DVD, and they boned before the movie was over. The end.

WHITE WOMEN

A lot of white women love black men. White people are growing up fusing their culture with ours, and white women are not stopping at hip-hop music, clothes, and soul food.

Ninety-five percent of the white women I have met have approached me first. Back in the day I would politely dismiss them, because normally we would have nothing in common. The eighties and nineties model of Becky would either be too dingy, sloppy drunk, or acting "too black" with her Cross Colours clothes and Salt-N-Pepa hairstyle, to be taken seriously. But the "New Millennium Becky" is no longer approaching black guys with off-beat dance moves and flat asses. The new Becky not only buys your drinks (something they've always done), but she is now comfortable in her own skin (she knows she's just a white girl that likes chocolate). She can "lean with it, rock with it" on the dance floor. And some white women now have backsides that would make Yao Ming say, "That can't be real!" and sistas saying "Daaamn, Becky."

Speaking of interracial mingling, can we all stop tripping about it? Regardless of what our personal preferences may be, the fact is dating outside the tribe is not the taboo it once was, and plenty of brothers *and* sisters are crossing color lines to get the love they need. And for black women who are already feeling like benchwarmers in the game, because they're not meeting any good black men, hey, meeting a white guy is an option you may want to consider. Hell, life is short and if you find a man who loves and treats you right, race doesn't have to be an issue.

And let's all stop grittin' and mean muggin' on one another when we see one of us with a member of the opposite sex who happens to not be black. First of all, you don't know the nature of their relationship. You never know—they could be business associates or even in-laws. Second, staring and giving them the evil eye is so rude and childish. Third, mind your business. This goes for men and women.

ALL-STARS

Now, I know most women could care less about dating a celebrity or an older successful man, but just in case you are approached I thought I'd fill you in on what I've learned. I hear women say all the time that every man is the same no matter who they are or what they do. That is a bunch of bs. You can say what you want, but until a famous person or a successful older man tries to talk to you, you don't know how you will react. When men have a life and career that allows them to choose from a wide variety of women, the chosen woman will not treat him the same as she would treat Ricky from the shoe store. I don't care what you tell me. I have seen women call famous guys cute, sexy, and fine, just because they are great actors, recording artists, pro-athletes, pastors of big churches, principals of schools, CEOs of companies, or funny comedians. (Ha, ha!) Fame or a lot of money makes women look at men differently. Period!

It all becomes the same, though, after a while. Once you get to know that person and have bonded and connected and done other things, no matter who we are or what we do for a living, the fame thing flies right out of the window, and we soon become the guy that either treats you good, bad, or the same as every other boyfriend. There are just more benefits (and some unique obstacles) that come with dating someone in the limelight or someone with authority and power. So take all that into consideration when you approach and/or are approached by someone you think is special or different, because of who he is or what he does for a living.

Now say you just met someone famous, and he is in town for the night or weekend. He expects you to sleep with him that night or you think he expects you to sleep with him that night. If you are only in it for a one-night stand (please read Chapter Five first), then it's up to you how you handle yourself—you can act as giddy and as starstruck as you want.

Just don't expect something more no matter how great the sex was and what he said to you afterward—even if he claims he has never said it before.

The Bottom Line ······························

It is easier said than done, but the best way to avoid getting mistreated or taken advantage of by a "baller" who tries to talk to you is to remain cool, cool, and then cool. You should never show a man you are overly impressed with his looks, fame, money, power, or even his interest in you. Just play it cool, if you can. He will think something is wrong or different about you when you don't go gaga over him, like everyone else. That will either impress him or make him move on to someone he can easily give goose bumps to. On the flipside, if you overly flattered a man before he proves to you that he is worthy of flattery, no matter how close you two get, he will never treat you as his equal. In short, he will run all over you. At the end of the day, men fall for women who bring something to the table besides generosity and good sex.

Fin-Diddy's Dating Pointers ·················
FIRST DATE, LADIES?

Remember, your safety and comfort should come first. If anything ever goes wrong on a first date, it's usually because the man has done or said something aggressive or neither of you are feeling each other. Therefore, I highly recommend that you come prepared with an out. Taking separate cars on the first date is a must. You can leave when you need to, and you won't become a hostage. Otherwise, when things are going bad, you are thinking, *Please just take me home.* And we are thinking, *Damn, I gotta take this chick home.* If you don't bring your own car, beware because there are some brothas that will leave you stranded. You gotta pay for the meal *and* call your cousin to come get you. Damn!

GOOD FIRST DATES
• Coffee, breakfast, brunch, lunch
Quick meals are good for first dates. It is noncommittal and you can get in–get out, if it is going bad. If it is going good, you still have the rest of the day, and you both can decide when and where the date should resume.

• Bowling
It's fun and you get to talk to each other without feeling rushed. You get to watch each other concentrate and bend over the whole time. You can also find out how competitive the other person is, if they can take being teased, and if they have a sense of humor. It's fun when you get a strike; funnier when you roll a gutter ball. If the date is going bad, it's over when it is over.

• Roller Skating

It is similar to bowling, but you get to hold hands. It also gives you plenty of time to talk, because you're either skating around the rink, sitting down and watching others show off their skills, or helping each other off the floor after an unexpected fall. Make sure to pick a good night to go. Ask about the night's music/theme first, because bad music can turn a good night horrible, really fast. But remember, eat at your own risk, because food at skating rinks sucks, and if you have to use the restroom, hold your breath. They rival gas station bathrooms in their degree of foulness.

• Arcades

Where else can you eat, drink, compete, and feel like a teenager again? It's great to win, but losing is not so bad either. And talking trash while playing games that require more physical exertion (think air hockey) can be downright sexy. Plus, you can leave whenever you want. How's that for a win-win situation!

• Outdoor Dates

Outside dates can be very fun if you like the outdoors. You can take a walk in the park or go biking. But do not have a picnic, because it's way too intimate for a first date. Just enjoy the scenery, the greenery, the sunshine, and each other. But if you are allergic to grass, sunshine, fresh air, squirrels, walking, and simply taking in all the wonders that God has created for us to enjoy, this is clearly not the first date for you. And if you're the kind who only uses outside to make your way inside, don't even bother.

There are many more places to go for first dates. Ask for recommendations from friends or check newspapers and the Web to find out about places or events that interest you *and* your date. A lot of men and women will want to make the destination of their first date a surprise, in order to expose the other to something new, but this can backfire. Why? Well, say a guy surprises you with horseback riding and you show up wearing a minidress, are afraid of horses, allergic to hay, and are repulsed by the sight and smell of mounds of manure. It would be hard to salvage the date and not think of him as the Animal Planet man from then on. My advice: keep it simple.

Then there are certain activities and venues that are fun, but that are not right—for now. Here are some of my thoughts on places and activities that you should avoid the first time you go out, but should save for later, when you know each other better.

BAD FIRST DATES (BUT GOOD LATER-ON DATES)
• Amusement Parks, Fairs, and Ghetto Carnivals
Amusement parks are fun, but they are also all-day events. You risk the possibility of one of you having unpleasant mood

swings before the date is over. Also, being in large crowds; waiting in long lines; and being around hordes of screaming kids who are pumped up on Coke, cotton candy, and sheer adrenaline doesn't allow you to focus on each other. Or you may be forced to come up with dialogue during those times you have to wait a long time to ride a roller coaster or buy overpriced junk food. Lulls in conversation are fine once you know a person, but in the beginning they're just plain awkward. Moreover, if you're having a great time, you could mistakenly think he's a great guy. Conversely, if you are not having a good time, you'll only blame him for taking you to a dumb theme park. Not to mention the fact that he's hell bent on riding Thunder River, and you'll be damned if you get your hair wet for anybody on the first date.

• Movies

Movies are bad first dates, because you never get to talk to each other, unless he likes to talk during the movie, which is annoying and should be grounds for an immediate end to the date. It's also possible, as with amusement park dates, to confuse a good movie for a good date, and seeing a bad movie can make you feel like you're on a bad date.

You want to be sure you like him *before* you sit together in a dark room, watching Denzel or Will Smith. It's a buzz kill to get all emotional, absorbed in Will fighting to keep his son, then look over to your left and think,

"Who is this clown?" Go on a movie date later, with someone you want to chill and cuddle with.

• Dinner

Contrary to what you may think, dinner is never, ever a good first date. There is just too much pressure. First, you have to decide on a place with food you both enjoy. Once you're there, it can be long and boring if no one is saying anything or the conversation is forced. Even if things are going well, you might have too many expectations or start feeling nervous about how the night will end. And heaven forbid he chews with his mouth open, eats off your plate, or exhibits any other off-putting behavior.

By the time the check comes, there is a whole new set of pressures to contend with.

He worries that:

- if he suggests going Dutch, you'll think he's cheap.
- if he pays, you may not be interested in him beyond the free meal he's providing.
- he may not have enough cash to cover the bill, considering you ordered the most expensive entrée on the menu, *plus* drinks, an appetizer, and dessert.

You worry that:

- if you suggest going Dutch it will set the tone for future dates, and he'll always expect you to cover half of everything.

- if you offer to pay, it might be perceived as an emasculating power move.
- if he pays now, he'll expect you to pay later. In bed.

I told you this was pressure.

• Poetry Slams

You'll hear all night that black women are queens and black men are statistics. Enough said!

• Concerts

The artist performing may be more of a draw than the person taking you. Personally, if the artist is Prince, Jill Scott, or Outkast, I would go with lazy-eyed, one-foot Felicia if she asked and would happily carry her to the concert on my back.

• Bookstores

Boring, unless you are buying my book.

First-Date Behavior ·······················

First dates are an opportunity for you to mention any fears, concerns, or bad date experiences. But keep those stories short! (I mean *short!*) You don't like it when men tell boring, self-indulgent stories, and we don't like it when you do it either. In fact, we listen very closely (in the beginning) and are quick to turn your story into an "it's not him, it's you, girl" CliffsNotes summarization. So don't give us any rope to hang you with. But providing us with a short story about your date from hell lets us know what not to do and where not to take things. Men need all of the inside information they can get when it comes to figuring out what puts you in a good or bad mood.

And speaking of information that affects a person's mood, here are three subjects that you should avoid altogether on the first date:

- Marriage—The first date is not the time to talk about the fairy-tale wedding you've been planning since age six. Nor should you talk about how all of your friends are either engaged or married. We don't care, and it scares us.
- Your kids—Talking about them is not good first-date conversation. If you have a child, it should be brought up before the first date. Some women feel like they have to keep it a secret, or it's none of our business unless we stick around. But I must say, the majority of women I know with kids are pretty upfront with it. A man asks, "What's your name?" She answers, "Two girls, what's yours?" It's okay. We want to know. Men will still date you.
- Sex—Don't even bring it up. If we bring it up—'cause we'll take it there in a heartbeat and end up ruining the date—direct the conversation to your comfort level or get us off the subject.

BEFORE WE SAY GOOD NIGHT

If you are feeling a guy on the first date, tell him! "I am having a nice time. This is going better than I thought." We will instantly be both flattered and slightly offended, but it will spark a fun conversation. If a woman told me that, it would make me say "I'm glad that you are having a good time but why would you think you would have a bad time with me?" (Then in my head I would think, *I'm the shizznit!*)

Always aim for a smooth ending to the first date, even when it—or he—did not meet your expectations. It could have just been an off night, or maybe he really is awful, but do not think it gives you license to be rude. Kindly thank him and part ways.

If everything went well on the date, don't get caught up playing cool. We interpret that as you not being that interested and you're just trying to end the night as quickly as possible. Now is not the time to shut down and say nothing. Rather than let it end with "I'll call you later," say you had a good time and offer to pick the place for a next date. We'll like to hear that.

Make plans for the second date at the end of the first date. Pick a place where there are few distractions and where you can talk, talk, talk. Get to know each other for real. Slide in even more of your interview questions and be more intimate, i.e., touching hands, hugs and holding, soft kissing. Space it out, but don't be afraid of invading each other's space.

I know I like it when a woman is assertive. "I like you! I want to get to know everything about you! I will more than likely give you some sooner than later, but not right now." If a woman said that to me, or even just treated me like that without actually saying the words, I'd be cool with that.

Kissing is definitely a go in the new millennium. If you really like him, it's cool to kiss on the first date. Men will not think you are easy. If you had a good time, are attracted to him, and you want him to know you like him, kiss him! As for sex, well, we get to that in the next chapter, so hold your horses.

The Bottom Line

Remember, if you barely know the guy, go someplace where you feel safe and comfortable and get to know him. Let the first date be an introduction. You want to go somewhere you can talk to the person and leave quickly if things are not going well.

Why Some Men Don't Call Back

So you had a good first date, but he didn't call back, and now you want to know why. Men are men and most of their actions and behaviors have not changed from when your great-great grandmother was having the same problems with Rufus. There are no ground breaking, cosmic revelations that will explain to women why men act the way we do.

With that said, ladies, there could be any number of reasons why he hasn't called. In that short time after your first date, he could have met and gone out with someone else that he is feeling more than you. The only reason he hasn't called to tell you is he wants to avoid that awkward phone call: "Hey, I know I said you were great, but I just met someone um, greater?"

Another reason could be a lover from his past is back in the picture. His ex-girlfriend sensed him being a little distant or preoccupied lately, so, since she is not ready to let go yet, she pops over to Rufus the IV's house to delay the process of him moving on. Ladies, while you are home, waiting for a phone call and trying to figure out how long you should wait before it's cool to give Rufus the IV a little taste, his ex is over at his crib making Rufus sing Negro spirituals.

Most men recognize the game. We know what the ex is up to, but she is at your house, talking dirty, wearing "those jeans," and going down a good street on memory lane. And she does that trick you like, followed by her smooth signature move, and um, errr, let's just say it's hard to say no to the ex. Now, where was I? Oh, he has totally forgotten all about you for the time being, and that "I'll call you tomorrow" has turned into weeks, sometimes months, until you break down and call him. And that's when Rufus answers the phone and hits you with the "Girl, your ears must have been burning, because I was just talking about you. Where have you been hiding?"

Tell Rufus he was on your mind and you're just touching base. If he has no real reason for not getting in touch with you sooner, use it as an opportunity to just say hi and bye. If he wants to prolong the conversation and hook up with you, don't rush back into something that turned out to be a big letdown. Let him know that if he is busy or dealing with other issues to go on and take care of business. Of course you want to hear someone say they like you and you are great, but more than anything you want them to prove it. Say straight up, "I don't have time for games and disappearing acts. Later, Rufus!"

Finesse's Call-Back Rule ·····················

You're allowed two calls, that's it! Never call someone after you have called them twice and have not gotten a return call. Call once and leave a message. If you don't hear back within two days, wait four to five days before calling again to say, "Hey, I called you, but I didn't hear back from you. When you get the time, hit me up." If you don't get a call back, never call again and move on, no matter what was said or how great the energy was when you met. *Two* calls, that's it. And in these days of caller ID, don't leave a message and keep calling back, hoping he'll pick up. The only thing that he'll pick up is that you're desperate.

If he was really interested in you, he would have returned your first call in no less than two days. If he calls you back after five days, he needs to have a good explanation as to why he waited so late to call you. You deserve an explanation, at least, and not some lame excuse, like "I lost my phone," or "I accidentally erased your number when I was deleting old numbers from my cell," or, my top favorite, "I had to leave the country on a top-secret mission, and now that we got the hostages back, I can concentrate on you. What's up?" You don't want a man you like thinking that it is okay to have you waiting around wondering if he is ever going to return the call. Don't put up with stuff like that.

The Bottom Line

Men who like you will call and will return your calls. If a man phones you once a week, or twice a month, or just sends you a text every now and then, he may like you, but he definitely has a woman he calls on a regular basis. Unless it's business related, give yourself a call-back rule with people you just meet and stick to it.

How to Win the Game

We all look for love and some of us get more chances than others to find exactly what we are looking for in a mate. A lot of women want to fall in love and get married, but first they have to find a man who loves them and wants to marry. In order to fall in love with someone who has mutual feelings, you must first build a strong relationship with that person. Before you can build a strong relationship with a person, you both have to go out on more than one date. In fact, you have to go out with that person a lot. Now, I know it's been said that some people have met that special someone, dated, fell in love, and married them all in one week. I don't know how long those marriages actually lasted before immigration stepped in, but for most women, perhaps like you, it will take many dates with different men until you find a good relationship that is going in a direction you find promising.

Don't be afraid to tell a man you went out with once that you are going out with other people. It's good for men to know that you have options and that you are not waiting for him to plan your weekend. It will give you a gauge on how serious he is about you and also how sensitive his jealousy meter is.

The reality of dating is different for everyone. Some women have no problem finding men who want to date them. Other women's opportunities come few and far between. Some women choose to date around, finding a lot of warm bodies in a bunch of cold-hearted men. Some women like to date only one guy at a time, hoping that he is the One.

Regardless of your situation, your goal in dating is probably the same: to find the One; a man who will love you and is willing to step up, unasked, when necessary. If that's not what you are thinking about when you are dating someone seriously, then that's what you *should* be thinking, because that's what a man is supposed to do. If black people don't know that, it's because a ton of us grew up with mothers or grandmothers doing damn near everything except providing the fertilization.

Let's continue to break this down from a male's perspective. If a man is not trying to be kept by a woman (meaning, he lives off of her), he should want to go out and do his best for himself, his woman, and his family. Now, for men, when it comes to dating, our ultimate, ultimate goal is to find a woman that we are attracted to ("I like looking at your face everyday."), motivated by ("I try my best to be on time for my woman. She does not deserve to wait."), and who provides nourishment ("My woman helps me grow, remain healthy, and keeps me strong.").

Lastly, a man wants to find a woman that he can comfortably provide for, according to her standards. I say that, because all men have their own standards. Some men set very high goals for themselves and bust their butts to achieve them; other men are not so motivated. If a woman's standards are higher than her man's, their relationship will not work out. If a woman wants the world, then there is no way a man can have a successful relationship with her if he just wants forty acres and a mule. But you should realize there's absolutely nothing wrong with him if he only wants a mule. That is his choice. It is perfectly all right for a woman to say I can't or won't date him, because I want more out of life. A woman who spends her time trying to convince a man that he should want more out of life is wasting her time. Leave him be. That man will try to convince you that there is nothing wrong with the way you two are currently living, or he will try it your way only to resent you if he fails. Focus your efforts on dating someone who wants similar things out of life that you do!

However, if you are willing to go down any road a man is traveling, because you have to have that particular man, just be okay with the fact that it could lead to steak and lobster or peanut butter and jelly. But if you have your own road you are traveling, one that leads to the things that are important to you, stop looking across the median rail at cars going in the opposite direction. Keep your eyes on the cars that are going on your side of the road. Those cars might be going faster or slower than you, but at least they are headed in the same direction.

CHAPTER FIVE

sex: when are relations-hip?

'Bout time you got here! This is my favorite chapter. For women, sex is a serious issue. You either *seriously* do it, or you are dead *serious* about not doing it, or you're *seriously* considering it. In this chapter, I'll tell you what men think about sex. By the time you finish reading this, you'll know the pros and cons of having sex on the first date; you'll be able to make the distinction between being a man's chill partner and being his girlfriend; and finally, you will know what questions ("Did you come?") *not* to ask immediately following sex, so you won't destroy the moment (we don't need no help doing that, we already got it covered). Now get to readin'!

After a string of nothing-to-call-home-about relationships, Donna met Ty and was immediately taken with him. His warm and engaging manner was an instant turn-on, and as they got to know each other, they found they had lots in common. Donna really liked how Ty seemed to be genuinely interested in her as a person, listening with rapt attention to her opinions and ideas. She admired the enthusiasm he brought to all areas of his life, be it his family, career, or hobbies. Hours spent talking on the phone evolved into wonderful dates when neither would want their time together to end. Before they knew it they had been dating exclusively for a month.

The physical attraction they shared for each other was so intense that it became harder and harder for them to part ways after spending time together. With feelings so strong, having sex was just a matter of time. The only problem was they both had different ideas on when that time would be.

In Donna's last few relationships sex had occurred fairly early. Afterward the whole affair would plummet into a downward spiral, much to her hurt and disappointment. Consequently she decided on the three-month rule: she would have to date a man consistently and exclusively for three months before she would have sex with him.

Ty, on the other hand, had a no specific rule, but he was tired of the recreational sex he'd been indulging in since he broke up with his last girlfriend a year ago. In his heart he was a one-woman man, and preferred an exclusive relationship. Ty felt that he and Donna had a good thing going, and it was bound to continue. To him, a month was more than enough time before becoming intimate. He didn't want to spend another moment on courting rituals and pleasantries. He was ready to do the deed and take their relationship to the next level.

Should Donna hold fast to her three-month rule and show Ty the door if he can't handle it, or should she throw caution to the wind and give him some? Can Ty reconcile himself to two more months of snuggling and cold showers, or should he just do a little creeping to get the sexual pleasure he craves from this chick he met a while back at the Super Wal-Mart? Stay tuned. . . .

Sex is a funny thing. It's physical and emotional. At best it can be loving, mind-blowing, comforting, and relaxing. At worst it can be boring, mind-numbing, upsetting, stressful, or the ever popular nonexistent. It can help to solidify a good thing, or if approached too casually or thoughtlessly, be the kiss of death for a new union. One thing for sure is that women and men view sex very differently. With that in mind, I'd like to help you better navigate what can sometimes be treacherous terrain. First, let's check out some of our basic ideas and differences on the matter:

THE FEMALE FACTS

- Women enjoy sex, especially when it's with someone they really like or are in love with.
- You feel if we really like you, we should wait until you're ready to have sex.
- Y'all really stress over having sex for the first time with a guy you like. If it occurs too soon, you agonize about

seeming too easy or being a victim of a "hit-'n'-run." If you wait, you worry about losing us to a more willing party.

- Like us, you like to get your freak on too. You don't need love or a relationship to do it. Hell, several of you don't even need a man—*some*body's buying up all those vibrators!

- You prefer sex steeped in romance—pretty lingerie, soft lights and music to set the mood (unless you creepin'.).

THE MALE FACTS

- Men enjoy sex. We will try to get it whenever we can, especially if we like you.

- For us, there's no proper window of time for a sexual relationship to commence; if you're down to do it on the first date, so are we. We were down before we picked you up!

- Men worry about saying just the right thing in order to have sex as soon as possible. We also worry about saying anything wrong that could delay it.

- We've always known that sex and love don't have to exist mutually. We can handle it as two totally separate entities, when never the twain shall meet.

- Sex has to be wrapped in the worst package for us to turn it down. Even then some of us will just close our eyes.

Women don't have to be so hung up on the sex issue. Either you want to do it with a guy or you do not. Whichever way, we like consistency. If we are never going to get it from you, and it is pretty clear we won't, we respect that and won't waste our time. We will continue to squeeze in some harmless flirting every now and then, to see if you've changed your mind, but that's it. Men would rather focus their efforts on women who "see us in that way." Sex is a really big deal for most men. The majority of us will tell you that it is among our top-three favorite things to do. Here's the breakdown:

1) Making money
2) Having sex
3) Eating or sleeping (it's a toss-up between these two)

By the way, this is the order of *my* personal top three, but don't expect other brothas out there to have their priorities as straight as mine.

When, When, When? ·

How long should you date a man before you have sex with him? I can't tell you. I am a strong believer that after a certain age (maybe twenty-two years old), things should happen naturally. Speaking for most men, if it feels right to you, it feels right to me. If it doesn't feel right to you, but you can tell it's feeling right to me, keep me vertical. Don't let me lay down anywhere and don't come sit on my lap to cuddle wearing, "those" jeans, sweatpants, short-shorts, or a short skirt. If it feels right to you, but for some reason it doesn't feel right to me, I won't be aggressive or make the issue of sex a big deal. I will wait.

When you decide to have sex for the first time, it should be a personal decision you make based on your values, beliefs, consideration, and heart. I've heard people say that they won't have sex before marriage. I'm sure that works for some people, and to those types, I say if you meet a man you like a lot, and neither of you believe in premarital sex, go on and get married, and move out of the way of the rest of us! And most men I know are not very religious when it comes to sex, and a lot of those who claim to be are the ones putting up the biggest front. I don't know too many women who actually abstain either. Okay, I know two.

Personally, if I am to be with one person for the rest of my life, we better know that we can please each other sexually for a long time to come. One reason married men cheat—and I'm not saying it's a good reason—is because their woman or wife doesn't do "that thing" they like, or she doesn't do "this" or "that" very well, or she totally stopped doing "that" completely. "Hell, I haven't had *that* since the night of lil' Rashaad's Christmas play over a year ago. I was wearing a blue sweater. It was chilly and drizzling a little bit that night. Yep, I remember that night." Believe it or not, some grown-ass men are moping around, talking that way to their boys. Here's a man secret I'll share: Depending on the severity of what's not being done in someone's love life, it is very customary for men to say a short prayer at night for their boys whose girls stopped doing "that." Anyway, having sex beforehand goes a long way in eliminating all that dissatisfaction later. And most times it's the woman who complains. Go figure.

When you're not dating, it's easy to say with conviction what you will and will not do, but once you're involved with someone, it's hard to put on brakes when you're nearly naked and he's found your erogenous zones. A wise person once said, "If you don't want to have sex, don't put yourself in a position where you're almost naked." I agree.

After you've told us you are not yet ready to take things to that level, we want you to mean it and prove it. Never put a man in charge of putting on the brakes when things get hot and heavy. We don't want that job, *ever*, and we will not do it. In fact, here's an example of how things can go when most men are assigned that job:

I GOT IT UNDER CONTROL, BABY!

Alicia and Jeff are lying in bed wearing only their birthday suits.

> Alicia: I thought you were going to be in charge of us not getting totally naked?
> Jeff: I'm not totally naked. I'm wearing a condom.

What you have to remember is that we've already assigned ourselves a job and what you want us to help you with is a direct conflict of interest with the task at hand, thank you very much.

And let me just say for the record that after a certain age there's nothing more pathetic than a grown-ass woman hunchin' with a man on the couch with no intentions of actually having sex. Don't act like you don't know what hunchin' is. You remember that how-far-can-we-go-without-actually-doing-it game that you and some boy played when you were young. You'd kiss and hump each other until your jeans faded and frayed. Where I grew up we called it hunchin' (big shout out ATL!). The idea of a woman getting herself and her man all worked up to the point of clothes being unfastened or removed, only to bring things to a screeching halt, is tired. And I hate those lame excuses you all give, like: "Okay, wait, wait, wait, wait, wait, whooooah! Okay, wait, we can't do this yet." Or the ultraconfusing I'm-saying-no-but-my-body-says-yes explanation:

"I don't want to stop because . . ." (as you kiss his neck) "I want you so bad right now . . ." (as your hand lightly brushes across his crotch) "but I have to stop . . ." (after he's worked your bra off). "Pleeeeease don't get mad." (You moan.) "I'll help you find your socks."

Uh-uh, that's whack! That's corny! It's so outdated, soap opera-ish, and trite. Any woman who continuously puts herself in that position with a man she really likes is playing games. Games, I say! You may not agree. Maybe you feel engaging in this type of behavior will make you more memorable to him, but I'm telling you that being a tease is not cool. While you're playing coy, you're also creating one upset and frustrated man. He may play it off to your face, but behind your back, he associates your very name with the word "frustration." Don't believe me? Well, check out this scenario:

THAT REMINDS ME . . .

Bobby and Stephan are playing Madden '07. A picture of Bobby's girlfriend, Karen, who he's been hunchin' for three months without hittin' it, sits on top of the TV. Stephan scores a touchdown and does a victory dance. Bobby slams the controller down.

> Bobby: That was luck! You know that wouldn't happen in a real game.
> Stephan: Aww, don't cry! Don't get frustrated.
> Bobby: I'm not getting frustrated. Oh snap! That reminds me, I have to go pick up Karen in twenty minutes. Put it on pause—I'll be right back.

I know, I know, it is definitely a woman's decision whether or not to go all the way. No means "no," and yes, he should always respect your wishes. You're right. You are absolutely correct. It's your body, and your body is a temple. Yep, you should be worshipped. I agree with all of that.

But just in case you're wondering what poor Bobby is thinking as he patiently waits for Karen to get a clue, here's some insight: He will start to think differently about her, and not for the better. Yes, he will respect her decision, but his feelings will go from admiration to frustration and possibly resentment. Yes, Bobby cares about Karen, but he may start creeping around, depending on his level of frustration.

FINESSE'S SUREFIRE COOL DOWN TIPS ·······

You're hugging, kissing, caressing, and undoing clothes. You've conjured up the mighty sex spirit, who's moaning, "Dooo it, dooo it!" in your ear. It might seem like you've reached the point of no return, but rest assured, here's what you can do to bring sanity back to the situation:

- Get up, walk around, and start cleaning (this is easier to do when it's your place).
- Ask him if he's hungry and make him some food.
- Grab a newspaper and start looking at the movie schedule. Then get dressed, insist he do the same, and head for the show.
- Ask him how his mother is doing. It's a low blow, but it's sure to put a damper on the mood.
- Or, like my grandaddy always said, "A hand job is better than nothing." (Sorry, he was nasty.)

FIRST-DATE SEX

The majority of women feel that it is never okay to have sex on the first date. It's just downright nasty, and it says a lot about a person's morals, up-bringing, and character. I can understand that. With all these diseases out there, not to mention encountering someone who's emotionally unbalanced, it's risky.

Do men frown on women who have sex on the first date? Sometimes. Do men turn down sex when it is offered to them on the first date? Not a very high percentage of us do, unless our mom is home and there is no place else to go. Is it ever okay to have sex on the first date? Yep! Sex on the first date is okay when two adults consent to it. They have discussed each other's intentions and fully understand that they may never see each other again. If a man and woman have bonded quickly in a way that leads to intimacy, that's understandable. People are human.

For example, say you meet a date at a park and you spend the entire day together, having a great time. As you walk around enjoying the scenery, you guys talk, laugh, and really get to know each other. As your comfort level increases, you may find yourself touching, holding hands, or even sharing a kiss or two. Later, you go to his place (or yours), make food together, and talk some more. Maybe you start watching a movie, but things heat up so much during the flick, next thing you know, you both look over and the TV screen is blue. Things are moving at a rapid pace, but are you prepared to accept the consequences that may come from sleeping with a man you're just getting to know?

If the answer is yes, make it clear that condoms are a must, even if he has to make a trip to 7-Eleven to buy some. Most important, after you've made the decision to do it, take responsibility for your actions. If you feel any regrets, don't come back to the man later, saying you really didn't want to do it or that he talked or coerced you into doing it. You're not being honest with him or yourself.

As men, we all like to think we can say something smooth or are just so overwhelming that women lose control and just give it up freely. But I know most women, before he says one word, can look at men and determine whether or not they would sleep with that dude. They just hope you don't say any-thing too stupid in the beginning to mess it up. I once asked a girl why she had sex with me on the first date. She told me that it felt right. She felt very comfortable with me, and she had not done it in a while, and she really wanted to. I asked her if she would have had any regrets if I never called her afterward. She said no, because she knew the chance she was taking and simply made a decision. Somehow I found myself more attracted to her after that response. It's refreshing that she was so honest and forthcoming.

When is it *not* okay to have sex on the first date? Probably when you meet a guy in a club and somehow end up at his place later on. Guys look at those occasions totally differently from the first example I gave.

If there is no emotional bonding whatsoever, no touching or moving moments shared, except what you did on the dance floor when Akon's "Smack That" blasted through the speakers, you just had a one-night stand. That is not cool if you roll like that on the regular. More than twice is really suspect. You are not going to find happiness from it, and you're potentially putting a lot of people at risk. You need to be safe and use condoms, because plenty of men look for women like you every time they go out at night (and day and late afternoons). Don't believe me? Here's the male perception:

The Freak

Jason and his roommate Chris are talking in the kitchen. Chris fixes a bowl of cereal.

> Jason: What did you do last night?
> Chris: I went to the club.
> (*They hear a loud thud from Chris's bedroom.*)
> Jason: What was that?
> Chris: Some freak.

Even if you never plan to take things that far, always use good judgment and common sense. One after party is enough if you go with a good friend, but hitting those after,

after parties is risky. I hate to hear stories of good women passed out, drunk, at the wrong time of night around the wrong type of guys. And since it's a numbers game, the more often you do it, the more of a chance something will go wrong. When you don't expect much for yourself, you can't expect much of anything from the guy you had sex with, who you barely know. Simply put, be careful!

A FRANK TALK ABOUT SEX ·····················

No doubt about it, sex is a wonderful thing. But if you don't enter a sexual relationship wisely, you open yourself up to all kinds of problems. There's unwanted pregnancy, all kinds of STDs, and what Prince tragically called "the big disease with a little name," AIDS.

Before you both get naked, make sure you're clear about where you both are sexually.

- Discuss your sexual history. You don't have to name who you've been with and where, but there should be an open conversation about things like whether there have been a few or many partners in your past, or if either of you had relations with the same sex. Do either of you engage in anonymous sex or sex with multiple partners? What sexually transmitted diseases, if any, have you encountered or been treated for?
- Talk about birth-control methods and determine which one works best for both of you.
- Always, always, always insist that your man wear a

condom, regardless of what he may tell you about his sexual habits or how "clean" he may appear. And don't always look to him to supply them—have your own stash of fresh condoms on the ready and make sure that you both know the correct way to use them.

• If your relationship progresses to the point of exclusivity, get an AIDS test. Go together for mutual support.

KICKIN' IT

We meet, we're both single, and we begin hanging out. We start fooling around pretty regularly. We're friends with benefits, late-night bumper buddies. We enjoy each other physically, with no strings attached. We're kickin' it.

Remember that song by Xscape from back in the day? ("Kick off your shoes and relax your feet, party on down the Xscape beat, just kickin' it . . .") Boy, those were women after my very own heart 'cause they got what kickin' it was all about. They were far ahead of the game at an early age. I miss those young ladies!

One situation that I see continually tripping up a lot of men and women is that they are having sex, like a couple, before determining if they are indeed a couple. These situations are like a crapshoot, because you're rolling the dice every time and taking your chances.

That's what was going on with Darlene and Bennie. They

started having sex after only a couple of dates. Darlene didn't have a problem with it at first, because Bennie always called the next day and they saw each other pretty regularly. He'd bring her little gifts or call her at work just to check in. As far as Darlene was concerned, theirs was a promising relationship.

What she was slow to get, however, was that getting together usually entailed sex. Sure, it may have started with a movie or a meal, but ultimately they'd end up in his bed or hers. Eventually Darlene tried to take things beyond their typical routine, which was beginning to make her feel bored and stifled. She would invite him out to parties with her friends or get-togethers with other couples she knew. He'd politely decline, but always encouraged her with, "Go 'head and do your thing, baby. Have a good time." Finally Darlene decided to have a *talk* with Bennie.

"What are we doing?" she asked him one morning as they snuggled.

"What do you mean?" he asked, confused that she would question what they normally did after sex.

"I mean, where is this relationship going?"

"Relationship? Um, I thought we were just hanging out."

Ouch! Darlene thought she and Bennie were on the same page, only to realize that they were reading from different books.

It never ceases to amaze me how some women who are looking for an exclusive relationship will have sex with a man first, then ask where they stand with him later. They're actually reluctant to ask up front. This is something you should approach just as pragmatically as you would other areas of your life. The same way you should never write a check without knowing exactly how much money you have in your checking account, or go on a road trip without knowing how much gas you have in the tank, is the same way you should approach having sex with a man. If not, you're destined for the type of ambiguity that leaves you with hurt feelings, time and time again. You'd like to assume that you're the only one he's having sex with, but you're not really sure, and you're not doing what it takes to find out. This is how the majority of just-kickin'-it affairs begin.

If you've ever found yourself in a just-kickin'-it situation and expected more, you're fooling yourself. Don't get mad that he didn't remember your birthday or take you up on that offer for Sunday dinner at your momma's. Y'all ain't rollin' like that. He doesn't consider you a girlfriend or a wife-y. The minute you feel your friendship taking a turn toward the bedroom, you need to say, "Listen, I'm not into casual sex. If I start doing it to you, I want to be the only person you're doing it with." If that is how you feel, then that is exactly what you should say. You were up front and made it clear to him before anything went down.

But here's a warning: Men view monogamy as being in a relationship, and we won't go for it if that's not what we want. We might go for the sex, but we won't associate it with monogamy. After you state your case, if he replies, "I don't want to be exclusive. I'm doing my thing and dating different people right now, but I totally understand where you're coming from and it's cool," he just told you that he is enjoying being single and that he is not going to change anytime soon. Remember, monogamy means absolutely nothing to a man who distinctly tells you this. He's also saying his relationship with you doesn't have to be a sexual one. He likes you. He enjoys hanging out with you, and he can be your friend. But understand, in the back of his mind, he's remembering you said you could have sex with him. He's not taking into account your stipulation. He's just concentrating on the fact that a possibility for sex with you exists. He's thinking, eventually, if he makes a move on you in a persuasive way, you'll drop your stipulation along with your drawers.

Say you two are having a great night chilling at his place, and you decide to have sex with him, despite your mandate that for sex to happen, you both had to be exclusive. Guess what? You just started having casual sex. You've made a decision based on "why the hell not?" You changed your position on the subject, but he didn't, and no matter how great the sex was or how close you two have gotten from that first conversation on the issue, unless you hear him say it—I *said*, unless you hear him *say* it—having sex with him once or on the regular from then on will not lead you to coupledom. You better believe that he is going to continue to date around until *he* is ready to settle down, so don't try to force him to limit his libido to only you or give him an ultimatum now that you're caught up emotionally.

It's futile for you to try to change us or tell us when we're ready for monogamy. We make that decision, and as most of you already know, men have no clue when that is. Believe it or not, one day we wake up and say, "I haven't been seeing anybody but you. Will you be my girl?" And she'll say, "Oh, silly, I haven't been seeing anyone else since the first night we went out. Of course I'm your girl." (Hee, hee, giggle, giggle.) I mean, that's pretty much how it will go down. Or guys will just start introducing you to other people as his girl and wait for you to correct him or confirm it. Or, if it was me, I'd say something, like, "Come here, love. Listen. You my woman! Now call all the guys in your cell phone and tell them you died!"

A man does not have to date only you, because you think he should. "I'm a great catch. What's wrong with me?" you may ask. Nothing. It ain't you. In fact, you could be perfect, but the timing is not. For whatever reason he's not pursuing an exclusive relationship right now. For him, sex is a different issue. He's not turning down sex if you offer it to him. Respect the fact that he told you how he feels and keep it real with yourself.

Men accept when women just want to hang out from time

to time. We don't know that much about your personal life, and the only thing you say if we ask you what's going on is, "I'm not ready for anything serious, I just got out of a bad situation." See! We all say that when, most times, the truth is we like you, we want to have sex, but that's about it right now. If you are a woman that likes to kick it, and all of a sudden you catch strong feelings for the guy you are kickin' it with, discuss it openly if you feel the need. But you have gotten him extremely comfortable with the present state of things, and most times a guy would rather go back to being just friends than start lying to you about exclusivity.

I know what I'm talking about here. I have done some things and have hurt some wonderful women for trying to pursue me when I was a confused mess, "focusing on my career" or just knew that I would not be faithful, so why lie. To those women, I am sorry for that, and I mean it with all sincerity. Men can be really inconsiderate, and a lot of women can write their own book on why they don't trust us. I also understand a lot of black men have not given black women much to have faith in.

But let's give some credit to the guys who openly admit they are players. If you are dating someone who just loves women and can't get enough of them, and does not appear to be slowing down anytime soon, you have to deal with that truth. Decide for yourself how much you like him and if it's worth sticking around to see how things will play out.

THINGS AREN'T EVEN STEVEN

Ever since Adam and Eve hooked up and snacked on apples, sex between the genders has never existed on a completely level playing field. Traditionally men have always enjoyed a type of sexual freedom that women haven't. Maybe it's because we can't get pregnant, or we don't worry about our reputations as much. If anything, having sex with a multitude of women can improve our reputations. Nobody ever called Wilt "the Stilt" Chamberlain a ho—not to his face, anyway.

These days, women are more sexually assertive, and I think it's a wonderful thing. It saves us a lot of guesswork when you're telling us how you want it, where, and when. Still, no matter how progressive and modern that approach is, our society still subscribes to double standards regarding sex, which can leave you a little vulnerable for guys to take advantage of. Think about it. Our culture celebrates a man's virility and his ability to woo several women at a time. Sure, some women may label such men as "dogs," but then they sort of resign themselves to the fact that men will be men. In fact, some women intentionally go after philandering types, hell bent on taming them (go figure).

Yet a woman who exercises that same kind of sexual freedom isn't cut the same amount of slack. Even in this day and age she's still labeled as "loose" or "promiscuous," and isn't viewed as marriage material. That's because a man doesn't want to think about who else you may be having sex with besides him, even when the relationship is not exclusive. The thought of y'all sleeping around just don't set right with us. Remember Nola Darling, the protagonist in Spike Lee's film *She's Gotta Have It*? She was messing around with three guys who were vying for her affection, and when they each found out they weren't the only one in her life, it drove them completely bananas.

Personally I don't think it's a good idea for a woman to approach sex the way guys do. It will screw up your head. Men can detach themselves from the physical act of sex a thousand times better than women. Have you ever had sex with someone, but did not kiss once? Think about it. It is in a woman's makeup to be emotional and nurturing. Men view sex as getting something. Women view sex as giving something. If a woman mentally feels like she is giving up too much, she would probably lose a sense of self-worth, identity, and often will need a man to help define who she is as a person. That's not healthy.

THE CONCLUSION

Let's now return to Donna and Ty. They like each other enough to further their relationship. They've obviously had *the talk* to even know they feel differently on the subject of when to have sex. How should Donna proceed?

I think Donna should stick with her three-month rule. She shouldn't have sex with Ty before she's absolutely ready.

Don't bend for nobody, Donna! Ty can either respect her wishes or be out. If he leaves, she didn't need that horny, impatient brother no way. Good riddance, Ty!

But I also don't think that Donna should have told Ty about her three-month rule. *Never* tell a man you have a set time limit before you'll sleep with him. Why? As soon as we know that, it's all we'll think about. That's not good, because it totally takes our focus off you and from enjoying your company and getting to know you better. Another disadvantage with time limits is that if we stop liking you between now and then, those of us who are immature will still hang around anyway to have sex with you after the limit is over. We'll have sex with you a couple of times, even though we know we're not going to stick around. You'll think it's all good then—*poof*—just like Kaiser Soze in *The Usual Suspects*, we're gone. So if you have a waiting period before you jump a man's bones, keep it a secret. Try and hold him off from knowing about it until you reach go time, unless you decide to break your own rule and break him off a lil sumthin', sumthin'.

The Bottom Line ························

The irony of sex is that we will strip down naked and do one of the most intimate things you can do with another person, yet be afraid to have an honest dialogue about what it is we're doing and what it means to us. Women and men alike will make all kinds of assumptions about where the other one is coming from, and when disaster strikes—like contracting a disease or dealing with an unwanted pregnancy or finding out there is a wife or a husband that the person "forgot" to mention—there's a lot of blame and resentment thrown around, without anyone considering what they did to get themselves into those situations.

THE AFTER-SEX TALK *NOT* TO HAVE ··········

Warning: The following are conversation starters you should definitely avoid after lovemaking—unless you want him to leave.

- "So what happens next? Are we dating now?"
- "Do you think we should have used a condom?"
- "Do you like kids?"
- "I'm so confused right now."
- "Why don't you want a girlfriend?"

CHAPTER SIX

should you go or should you stay?

There's an old saying that goes, I can do bad by myself. What it means is that in matters of love, you don't need to be with a person who's going to drag you down in the mud or rake you over the coals. Life is hard enough without the person who is supposed to be the love of your life, disrespecting you or offering you little or no support.

I always hear black women voice the I-can-do-bad-by-myself line when they are referring to some no-good man who trampled all over their heart. Unfortunately they'll say it, but I don't see a lot of them who are in bad situations actually doing something to fix it. It's one thing to recognize the negativity, monotony, selfishness, cheating, abuse, and general unhappiness that come from being involved with the wrong person, but it's another thing to take charge and make a positive change. Why do some of you allow so much hardship in your relationship and your life? What gives?

If I didn't know any better, I would think that women are compelled to go through drama when it comes to their love lives. Some of you will put a lot of time and energy into the wrong man for the sake of having a man. You get so caught up in his craziness that you never seem to make happiness and fulfillment a necessary part of your equation. Or worse, you begin to accept his craziness as normal or something that you deserve.

You'll know he's full of crap, but hang in there with him, anyway. A whole year will go by, and he's still spending your money, not being totally honest, and he certainly doesn't have your best interest in mind. Sometimes a man's very own mother, if she really likes you, will advise you to save yourself and run. But there you go, compromising your morals, integrity, and self-respect, because you're afraid of being alone. Some of you actually think you have to stick in there and change him, or save him from himself.

By now you should know good and damn well you can only change your *choice* of men, not the men themselves. You'll never find a good guy if you're too busy working on a bad one. I say, let that brotha drown! He should have learned to swim before he hooked up with you.

I've found that there are three primary reasons why women stay in bad relationships:

1) **Children**. You have a child or chillrenz with him. Even though he's a lousy mate, he's a good father. You stick with him, because you don't want your child to grow up not knowing who their daddy is.
2) **Finances**. If you had the money, you would be out of there in a heartbeat. But you can barely afford to pay attention let alone move out on your own. Your basic survival is dependent upon ol' dude. Besides, you don't want to have to downgrade the lifestyle you've become accustomed to, especially if you're dating a man with dough. Who wants to return to their meager existence and start all over after dating Daddy Warbucks?
3) **Loneliness**. You can't stomach the thought of being by yourself. Besides, the guy you keep on the side, because your man is a jerk (let's keep it real), can only keep you satisfied up to a point. He isn't enough for you on a full-time basis.

I know women who have been dating Mr. Wrong for so long, it is hard for them to know up from down without him pointing out the direction. And let's face it, some of you are so caught up in who you are with a man, you never consider the person you might have to become without one. Others of you have resigned yourselves to living a lie. You work hard at maintaining an idyllic facade for the public, even though things between you and your man are anything but ideal.

A friend of mine who dates a big-time investment banker is a fine example of just that. She admits she's in a relationship she should have left a long time ago, but according to her, "If it looks like you are living a perfect life, the last thing you want to admit is that your life is not perfect. I don't have the energy to fight with him about leaving, or fight with my friends and family about the reasons they think I should stay. I'm damned if I do, damned if I don't. It seems I am staying in a bad relationship for everyone but myself." That's sad.

While she's staying for the financial and lifestyle benefits that her man with money can provide her, there are a lot of women out there who bring home the bacon, fry it up, serve it, then clean up afterward without a bit of support or a word of appreciation from their men. Instead they hear about how they're slacking or not doing enough to help them. The complaint that I've been guilty of using once or five times is, "If you were more supportive, I could get out of this rut and get back on my feet." In a relationship where a woman is taking care of business and providing for both of them in a way that the man isn't, the man can come to resent the woman and lash out, because of his own insecurities and frustrations. It's senseless and immature, but it's real.

All relationships have their ups and downs. Some are keepers while others are simply not worth salvaging, no matter how much you think you love him, how much he says he's willing to try, or how long you've been together. But some people want to jet over the pettiest things, like, "Didn't I tell you yesterday to leave the cap on the toothpaste? I'm out!" Other people will hang in there and endure a whole lot of ridiculous bs, because that's what they think love is supposed to be about. You'll hear: "I'm sorry I came home early and caught you cheating on me with the coworker I introduced you to at my company's Christmas party. Next time I will call first. You know you wrong, but I'm a good woman and will stand by you while you try to work this cheating out of your system. I know it's hard, but I got your back, Boo."

So when *should* you stay and try to make it work, or pull up stakes and be out? Read on.

Almost Married

When Sunny hooked up with Trent, she thought the sky was the limit. He had big dreams, big ideas, and all he talked about was the great life they were going to have together. Trent made everything sound so rosy, Sunny moved in with him and started planning the wedding before he popped the question, which he still hasn't. Two years have passed, and they are no closer to an altar than when they met. Should Sunny stay, walk, or run?

If Sunny's goal is to marry Trent, the first thing she has to do is clearly and precisely state her intentions and tell him why it's important to her. Maybe this is just the nudge Trent needs to get moving. He could be the kind of person who sees the big picture—in this case, married life—but doesn't quite know how to deal with the details of actually planning a wedding and making it happen. In this case, Sunny should sit down with him and draw up a plan and schedule for their nuptials, then delegate tasks between them. She should give him manageable tasks that are pretty straightforward and don't require a whole lot of decisionmaking, like reserving the church and reception hall or checking limousine rates. She should not put him in charge of selecting the caterer or picking out floral arrangements. We don't know nothing about place settings, and beyond roses and daisies, our knowledge of flowers is limited.

Perhaps Trent is reluctant, because he feels like everything has to be just right before he makes Sunny his wife. A lot of men want their (financial) affairs to be in perfect order—be it having a decent job or making a good salary—before making the big commitment. That's commendable, but don't let him use money as an excuse not to move forward. Since things are seldom perfect, this kind of man has to learn to be flexible. If money is an issue, maybe a simple ceremony instead of a lavish affair is a better option. (It's never a good idea to put your future happiness at stake by incurring huge debt from a wedding you cannot afford. Doing that blows up in your face every time.) They could also cut back on spending in other areas of their lives to better afford a wedding. Does Sunny really need to buy a pair of shoes every week? And maybe Trent could start drinking domestic beer instead of that expensive imported stout he's been guzzling. If he's got a gut, he could reduce his spending and waistline by passing on the beer altogether. None of these situations are too complicated to resolve. Sunny should stay.

But if she determines that Trent is all talk and is just stringing her along so she'll continue to iron his shirts and pack juice boxes in his lunch, then she needs to walk. Even though she's invested a significant amount of time into this relationship, the reality is, there are no dividends to be reaped here. It's a waste of time to stick around with hopes that he'll come around.

The Bottom Line

Once you start living together, it is very easy for a man to get comfortable with the way things are. We can get so used to the perks of this marriagelike arrangement we don't want to mess it up by actually getting married. That's when you women have to take charge of the situation.

The Thrill Is Gone

Keisha and Andre's relationship used to be on fire when they first got together, but now it's just lukewarm. Andre's a nice guy and Keisha loves him dearly, but, sexually, he hasn't done it for her in a while. She increasingly finds herself fantasizing about other men and is afraid she may eventually act on it. Should she stay, walk, or run?

Keisha has to figure out what it is about Andre's lovemaking that has changed for her. Has he become lazy in bed, leaving her to do all the work? Maybe it's not him at all. She could be so stressed out over work or helping her hardheaded sister find a job that she can't fully enjoy all the pleasures Andre serves up. Either way, Keisha should tell Andre they need a Red Bull energy shot in their love life and discuss ways to get the sex back on track.

In these types of situations it's best to leave no stone unturned. They can explore options, like role-playing, sex toys, romantic getaways, new positions, new places, books, sex tapes or DVDs—whatever it takes to spice things up. Keisha has to be sensitive in her approach, however. She doesn't want to risk insulting Andre, turning him off or making him think she's getting all these bright, new ideas from another guy. She should stay, keep the lines of communication open concerning sex, and try to work it out.

Keisha's sexual fantasies about other men are not necessarily a bad thing. She could use those images to help rev up things between her and Andre. However, if for whatever reason she is no longer attracted to Andre and wants to pursue other options, she should just walk away and not cheat on the dude. Time away from Andre may make her realize that he's the love of her life, she made a horrible mistake, and return to him. Or she may meet someone who blows her back out and makes her say, "Andre who?"

It's All About Him

Cheryl was crazy about Jeff, a successful artist she'd been dating for six months. He took her to fancy galleries, fine restaurants, and introduced her to an exciting world of interesting people, places, and things she'd never experienced. The only problem is Jeff is all about Jeff. He never seems interested in her pursuits or passions, or cares much about what was going on in her life apart from him. Cheryl is starting to feel like an accessory in his fabulous world instead of his girl.

Here's how things go down between them:

OH NO, HE DIDN'T!

Cheryl walks into the house with a bandaged, sprained wrist. Jeff, in a robe and *Teenage Mutant Ninja Turtles* house slippers, is sketching a flowerpot. Cheryl stands beside him.

Cheryl: I got into a fistfight at work today.

Jeff: Move over! You're blocking the light.

Cheryl: My boss touched my bottom, and then winked at me when I turned around.

Jeff: From the bottom to the top. That's my girl.

Cheryl: Then he called me the N-word after I punched him.

Jeff: Speaking of the N-word, can you make me some noodles? I'm starving.

Cheryl: *Excuse me?*

(Cheryl then removes a shoe and flings it toward

Jeff. It whizzes by his head, missing him by an inch. She walks out of the room.)
Cheryl: Oh no, he didn't.

Cheryl had always hoped to be in a relationship where the support and attention she gave her man was reciprocated, but Jeff's self-centeredness is becoming unbearable. Should she stay, walk, or run?

Too bad Jeff hasn't learned that you can be a narcissist without being mean and rude to the woman you love. What he should have done was to gently caress her face, then gaze lovingly into her eyes while saying, "Cheryl, darling, I couldn't give a rat's ass about what goes on where you work. In fact, I am not very interested in what goes on in your little life, generally. But you do make one hell of a casserole, so why don't you stop yapping about your job and make me something to eat." Just jokes!

My advice to Cheryl: Don't try to work it out—*walk* it out. Pack your things and Van Gogh! Get it? Van *Gogh*. Go? Anyway, Jeff loves Jeff at the moment, and when you are that focused on your career and yourself, you have very little time for anyone else. Cheryl should be out.

He's Got a Secret

Every so often you'll hear something on the news about some guy who is living a double life—partaking in something unethical, illegal, weird, or crazy that his family and friends know nothing about. Most times it's something like he had a family or two on the side, and it isn't revealed until he dies, and his wives and children come forward to collect on his estate. Or you'll read something, like, "Kirk Franklin Addicted to Porn." What the hell?

Even scarier are those nondescript guys, usually from the midwest, who go off to work everyday, leaving behind an arsenal of war-worthy weaponry in their garages. We don't learn about them until something real bad happens, and the first thing their neighbors say is, "He seemed like a nice guy. I thought the reason he cut his grass with a machete was because he was Jamaican." You never know.

Nowadays, women are actually Googling men they're interested in to avoid any skeletons that may be in his closet. Can you ever know *everything* about the person you're dealing with? Probably not. Everybody's got secrets.

Nikki had been with Steve for two years, but had no idea he had a kid until a teenager tapped him softly on the shoulder at the mall and said, "Father?" Beverly thought Shane was handling his business until the repo man unceremoniously took his car as they were preparing to head off for a weekend trip. Stacie could have sworn her man Ed was drug free, until she unexpectedly arrived at his place one day, and he was stoned out of his mind. That's when she found out everyone in the neighborhood, including his own momma, called him "Weed Head Ed."

There are secrets, and then there are *secrets*. We all have some sort of information about ourselves we keep on the hush-hush, because we'd feel embarrassed or ashamed if loved ones knew. But sometimes deep, dark secrets that could hurt people's feelings come bubbling up to the surface in a relationship, do serious harm to their reputations, or put their safety and well-being in limbo. Your decision to stay, walk, or run depends on what that secret is. Here are some examples with my advice for you to consider:

1) **He has been to prison before for assault.** Stay or walk, depending on who he assaulted and why. If he assaulted his boss after working for a company for ten years, and they let him go at the end of the day for no reason, after the company became successful off of his hard work, ideas, and sweat—stay! That's just a little temporary insanity.

   If he assaulted a guy for disrespecting him or his family, stay, depending on how bad the guy was actually hurt. A black eye? Stay. A coma? Run! If he assaulted a cop over a traffic violation, walk. Every black man knows, when you hit a man in a uniform and who has a weapon, you are asking for jail, a beat down, and then jail again. He might be a little off his rocker.

   If he assaulted a woman for any reason, run! Men must never hit women! Never! Some women can act like men and hit like men when it comes to volatile confrontations. However, a man should never hit a woman; he should get his sister to do it!

2) He can't read. When one of us is illiterate, we all look bad. But you also have to question what kind of circles you're hanging out in to attach yourself to a man who can't get through a volume of Meet Dick and Jane. But stay! My motto: Each one teach one. Pull out the primers and teach homeboy to read. Have him watch top-notch educational shows, like *Sesame Street* and *Reading Rainbow.* Tell him he can't make love to you until he's read you at least one story straight through without stumbling on the hard words. He'll be as smart as President Bush in no time!

3) He likes your best friend. Stay, but know that one of them has to go. If she's your BFF who's been with you through thick and thin, give him the boot, because good friends are hard to find. If she's a temptress and made overtures that got his attention in the first place, get rid of her, because she's not really your friend. Finally, if he's determined to make moves on your buddy, and she's taking him up on it, leave both their asses alone, because they deserve each other.

4) He is addicted to porn. Stay! In the scheme of things, that ain't so bad. I was too for about a month; I got over it once I was old enough to get into strip clubs. Problem solved!

5) He has a substance-abuse problem. With black people it depends on the choice of drug as to whether we stay, walk, or run. If it's green, don't be so mean. Take flight if it's white. And if he needs a needle, syringe, spoon, lighter, and that thing to tie around his arm to make his vein pop up, *run*—and get him help or an audition for HBO's *The Wire*.

6) **He has a gambling problem.** Stay, but only if he wants help and makes a concerted effort to get it. Walk, if not. Run, if he wants to borrow a large sum of money, or if he's nickel-and-diming you to death.

7) **He is a drug dealer.** Walk! You are endangering yourself every time you go out or ride around in his Cutlass Supreme. Whether it's a rival drug dealer or the police, you never know who might be after him. But try not to run. He may think you squealed on him to the police and come after you.

8) **He lied about his name, age, and job.** Run. With an MO like this, he's hiding from more than just you. And you might want to call immigration while you're at it—or *America's Most Wanted*!

9) **He likes to wear women's undergarments.** Stay. And take pictures. Then walk with the pictures. You can use them for blackmail every time you're low on the rent. (What up, Marv Albert!)

10) **He has a child you didn't know about.** Stay or walk, depending on his reason for not telling you about his child. Who knows? The kid could be a government spy and he was only trying to protect his identity.

11) **He has herpes and never brought it up.** Walk! This type of information should be known well before having sex.

12) He has slept with more than three hundred women.
Stay if his penis still works. But make sure he stops, as long as you two are a couple. (I know many of you are thinking, *Eewww! That's nasty.*)

13) He steals grapes from the produce section of the grocery store. Run. That's just crazy!

Cheaters

Ricky had been ripping and running so much for his job, he forgot to make arrangements for a dog sitter before heading off on his next business trip. When his girl, Jan, said she would take care of feeding and walking O. J., he handed her his keys and boarded the plane with the satisfaction that he could count on her.

What he hadn't counted on was nosey-ass Jan had scrolled through the numbers on his caller ID, and noticed a certain out-of-state number appearing an inordinate amount of times. Before she knew it, she was dialing those digits to find out who exactly would be on the other end of the line. When a woman's voice answered, her heart immediately sank, and she got that big lump in her throat, but she had to know.

"I'm calling for Mr. Richard Banks," she said in her best business tone.

"He's not here," the woman replied tersely, adding, "and he will no longer be staying here. Please don't call again, nosey-ass Jan. Yep. I know it's you. I know all about you. I have caller ID as well, so when Richard's number popped up and it was a girl's voice pretending to be a professional, I instantly thought, 'This is nosey-ass Jan.' I figured you might call me one day, because Richard is not that bright. I'm surprised it took you so long to figure it out. I guess birds of a feather . . . Hold on for a second while I hang up!"

Jan got her answer and then some. Should she stay, walk, or run? I say run, Forrest, *run.* But don't forget to feed O. J. the dog before you go. . . . He's innocent. Oh, and don't let anyone talk to you like that on the phone or anywhere else. You gotta go find this trick and give her a beat down just on GP ("general principle" for my slang-challenged readers).

Cheating has become so commonplace these days, it's no longer viewed as the serious violation that it is. From the businessman who messes around with his secretary, to preachers who prey on, rather than pray with, female members of their congregation, to any number of celebrities who've been caught in the act, we've grown accustomed to it being a possibility in our relationships. Maybe it's because, aside from temporary embarrassment, it doesn't seem to really be bringing anybody down. Remember, we had an acting president admit to having an affair with an intern, and his popularity ratings are still high. Dollar, dollar Bill y'all! It's almost like cheating isn't the crime; getting *caught* is. That's why that advertisement declaring "What happens in Vegas, stays in Vegas" is so popular. It wittily sends the message that there's a place where you can sneak around and not get caught.

But on the real, cheating has to be one of the most deceitful and selfish acts a person can do to their partner. For a person to profess their love for someone one minute, then lay up with another person when the opportunity presents itself, is just plain low-down. Relationships are built on trust, and you can't trust a person who cheats, no matter what excuses they may have for why they did it. Have I ever cheated on a girlfriend? Yep. Have I ever been cheated on? Yep. I have hurt and been hurt. Neither feels good. Especially when a person has been wronged, but who did everything right.

Yet there are a lot of women who will tolerate it for various reasons. Some of you file it under the men-will-be-men category, like cheating is actually in our DNA and you have no choice but to tolerate it. Others may turn a blind eye to a man's philandering ways, because they enjoy the perks of his professional or social stature, or the sex is really great. One woman I know who dated Pretty Ricky admitted to me, "I just figured cheating comes with the territory with pretty boys. I look at it as the price I pay for being with somebody who looks so good!" She lost me there. I don't think most men would tolerate a fine-ass cheater, even if she looked like Saana Lathan. But, hey, chalk it up as another difference between the sexes.

The fact of the matter is, all men don't cheat, and don't think for a minute that you have to be with one who does.

Do tread lightly in this area, however. Just because he comes home late doesn't mean he's been with another woman, and if he says he was hanging out with his boys, chances are he was. And don't be tripping off that sweet smell emanating from his shirt—it ain't no perfume; it's his new unisex cologne. In other words, don't go around being suspicious and firing off accusations unless you know for sure you're justified to do so. A hunch is one thing; paranoia is quite another, and you'll turn a good man, who's really trying to do right by you, off with that kind of hysteria. If a man never gets credit for doing right by you, what's the point of trying?

If you do find out he is cheating on you, there's still no need to fire off accusations, because now you have the cold hard facts. Address it immediately, tell him there's no room in your life for a cheater, and be out. Trust me, you won't come out a strong person in a relationship with a cheater. You'll be constantly scrutinizing his actions and motives, and second-guessing your own instincts and perceptions and self-worth, all of which will make you an emotional basket case. Who needs that?

On the flipside you find out that a man has a girlfriend or wife, because he *told you* he had one, but you continue to flirt and push up on him, he is either going to walk away, or stay and play. If he decides to play, because you didn't walk away after he told you his situation, you are not looking for a relationship. In fact, you are not even looking for a good guy. You are only looking for drama. Now, don't get me wrong. There are women who absolutely refuse to get involved with a man who is involved with someone else. Those women understand the drama, the hurt, and problems caused by cheating. Other women make it very easy for men to cheat. Just like there are men that are nothing but dogs, there are women who pride themselves on being dogcatchers.

Men often need no encouragement to cheat. The undeniable truth is that most men have a problem turning down free money and free sex. It is in our nature to hunt. But when men retire and put up the hunting gear or let their teeth and claws get dull, gazelles (that's you) come out of the brush, dancing around the cheetahs (that's us), like a merry-go-round. But there are a lot of good men out there who are happy in their relationships and hold their women down at all times whether they could possibly find out some dirt or never know. A lot of men won't cheat! They have integrity, they are focused, and they are happy with what they have at home, and have no desire to jeopardize or put at risk their family or relationship.

Infidelity always ends badly. Usually the third person gets caught up in an emotional, unstable love triangle, because she or he really starts having feelings for the person they can't openly be with. Then everyone ends up on *Jerry Springer*, waiting for the boxing bell to sound and the big white bald-headed guy to break up the scuffle. I think all that drama can be avoided if more women stopped allowing men to be selfish. If you approached him, and he said he was involved with someone but still wants to kick it with you and you go for it, then he is the guy that every woman hates and talks about, and you are the woman that has no right to complain about getting played or being done wrong.

When women turn a conversation with a man who is in a relationship or married into a what-she-doesn't-know-won't-hurt-her conversation, it always disappoints me. I have asked women why they don't mind being number two or three on a man's list when he clearly has a number one. The words I have heard used in their responses are "loneliness," "selfishness," "excitement," "passion," "neglect," "lust," "infatuation," "game," "naivety," "boredom," "misled" (as in he said he was going to leave her and be with me), "settling," "revenge," "love," "temptation," "curiosity," "opportunity," and "competition." I know women that justify their actions of being with married or involved men by saying, "well, if his woman was taking care of business at home, he would not have cheated on her in the first place." Not true! There are women who take care of so much business at home, they don't have time to run behind their man (who they do absolutely everything for) to see if he is acting right. Eventually we all have to take responsibility for our own actions. Cheaters too!

I know men have to be strong and take responsibility for themselves as well, but my point is that men are not the only villains in these cheating situations. It always takes two. A man who would have sex with a woman, with no strings attached, would not have that opportunity if women avoided those men who are charmingly trifling. If you both agree to go for it, so be it. If your gut and common sense tells you not to get pulled into any mess or drama, go with your gut feeling. Women often say "all men are dogs" but there would be less cheating among men if there was more sisterhood among women.

BEING THE OTHER WOMAN · · · · · · · · · · · · · · ·

"In the beginning, we met as friends. Next thing I knew, I wanted him to leave his wife. I thought he was not with someone that was his intellectual equal. He always complained how he and his wife stopped having sex. 'She does not do it for me,' he would say. 'She is not interested in the things I want to do. She has no motivation. She is not striving for anything.' He would take me out on real dates. Hell, sometimes, I forgot I was the other woman.

"One day I woke up, and then I *woke up*. He never told me he was going to leave her, and enough was enough. I was tired of it always being my place or . . . my place. I didn't come from that. I was better than that. I started going out with other guys—other *available* guys—and never looked back."

—S. G., thirty-one, New York

Being the other woman is a temporary high. It might be cool at first, while you are having fun. But realize that it will deflate as the reality of his situation starts to weigh on you. You are the other woman, not the woman. Face it. He will not be leaving his wife, kids, or dog for you!

Cruel Intentions

Shelly got up an hour earlier than she usually did for work. That's because she needed extratime to work some magic on the bruise left by Darnell's pimp-slap to her face the night before. As she dabbed on makeup to cover the bruise, all she could think was, *How in the world had things gotten to this point?* After all, she came from a good family, was well educated, and had a good head on her shoulders. How did she manage to hook up with a man who saw fit to go upside her head at whim, and more important, why was she sticking around?

Fran was feeling depressed and out of sorts despite being on her way to a family reunion that she had been looking forward to for months. Although she tried to cheer herself up by sporting a favorite outfit and listening to upbeat music, deep inside she was still reeling from the explosive argument that she and Kyle got into the night before. It started over something silly—as it usually did—and the more she tried to guide the conversation in a more constructive direction, the angrier he became. It ended with him berating her something terrible and calling her everything but a child of God. Now she's trying to put on a happy face for family, but his hurtful words still haunt her and are wreaking havoc on her confidence and esteem.

Toni would do anything for Troy, and he takes full advantage of that fact. Whether he's short on cash, wants her to prepare snacks for the card game he's hosting at her house, or letting him borrow her car that he's dented on more than one occasion, she supports her man even when it inconveniences her. *After all*, she tells herself, *you've got to take the good with the bad when you're in love*. But it's getting increasingly harder and harder to remember the good.

Shelly, Fran, and Toni are going through some serious stuff. Should they stay, walk, or run?

Love isn't supposed to hurt. Do you hear me, ladies? Love is *not* supposed to hurt. You have to come to terms with the fact you are in the wrong relationship with the wrong person. Yet on any given day we'll hear a news report about some man who's beaten or killed his woman, or overhear a guy describe how he had to physically put his girl in line. There are the lewd and disrespectful comments women endure from crazies they meet on the street, and the whack rap lyrics that degrade women on a regular basis. Misogyny, and the violence it can breed, surely exists out here, but that doesn't mean you have to cozy up to it.

Abuse refers to the physical or psychological mistreatment of a person. The scenarios I've described here are all examples of abuse. When a man makes unreasonable demands on your time and resources, when he calls you names, and certainly when he physically harms you, it is abuse, plain and simple.

The first thing you must do is to see it for what it is. I know it's a hard pill to swallow when someone you love is hurting you in this manner. Maybe you resort to blaming yourself for his ill behavior, or you beat yourself up for not detecting his craziness sooner. But don't go there. Men who engage in abusive behavior can be real charmers. That's how they got in with you in the first place. Unless you performed a serious background check, you have no way of knowing the man who seemed so caring when you first started dating could ever treat you so cruelly.

The second thing you have to do is promptly disengage from the relationship. This is no time for you to be having a stand-by-your-man moment. After all, he ain't really your man if he's looking to diminish rather than support you. He's already proved himself unworthy, and you deserve much better. Tell him clearly and unequivocally that you are calling it quits. Do not feel that you owe him an explanation; he knows what he did. And under no circumstances should you leave the door open for further communication, no matter how innocent it may seem, because you don't want to give him an opportunity to wiggle his way back into your life. Change your number, your address too, if necessary. Don't stay in touch with his friends, frequent his hangouts, or do anything else that will bring you face-to-face with him. Cut him loose and move on to higher ground. I know it's not easy, but believe me, the air is clearer up here and the view is beautiful.

If you have the slightest inkling that he may be out to harm you in any way, especially if he has physically done so before, don't be afraid to take out a restraining order. It's a formal line of defense, and hopefully he'll get the message that you will not stand for his abuse and leave you alone. It's also a good idea to inform your trusted friends or family members. I know a woman who e-mailed her ex's home and work address, home and work phone number, license plate number, and a brief synopsis of how he harmed and threatened her to her circle of good friends, just in case. These may seem like extreme measures, but I feel it's better to be safe and alive than sorry.

Finally, see an abusive relationship as the traumatic experience that it is. Don't think it's something that you can just sweep under the rug and get over. Not dealing with your psychological and emotional health after such a negative experience can impact your life, long after the initial hurt is gone, and make it difficult for you to develop a healthy relationship in the future. Don't try and shoulder this alone; get the professional psychological help you need for as long as you need it.

The Bottom Line ······························

It's tough sometimes to figure out when to stay, walk, or run. When it comes to certain problems and obstacles, women get impatient and bounce without even trying to work something relatively simple out, or stand by their man and his foolishness, to their own detriment. Don't let your heart, loneliness, or even fear make you stay in bad situations. Use good judgment and common sense when deciding if you should stay, back away, or run like hell from a bad situation. If it is meant to be, you can always pop back up on the scene after you have had time to step away from the trees and take a really good look at the forest. Men disappear and pop back up all the time, so don't feel bad for making sure you are doing what is best for you.

CHAPTER SEVEN
real love

Love Sick
by Finesse "Langston Hughes" Mitchell

I'm just a mess in Love.

And don't want to be cured when I'm sick in Love.

And when I hurt from Love,

Dropped to the earth by Love,

I'll still finish each sentence and SMILE, big in Love.

It's what you make it, Love.

So if you fake it, Love,

You'll probably be sick of it all, instead of sick in Love.

To me, dating is a journey that leads you to true love with that special person you want to be with for a very long time. But if you think the journey ends there, think again. Lots of times women view landing a man as the goal. You do what it takes to attract and meet him. Then you date and get to know each other. Something magical happens, and you both conclude that he's the one for you and you're the one for him. Besides, his momma likes you, and your dad feels he's a fine young man. Great! Now all you have to do is pick out a ring and china pattern and live happily ever after, right? Wrong!

If it was that easy, you wouldn't be reading this book. Before you start high-fiving your girlfriends and declaring, "Mission accomplished; Charles Romel Johnson is all mine!" realize that the journey has not ended. But we are entering the home stretch. The crucial remainder of the journey is figuring out what you both can live with for a lifetime and doing what it takes to nurture and maintain your relationship.

This is *not* the chapter to skim through or sweep under a rug.

Can We Talk? ·

I can't say enough about communication. It's the necessary thread for understanding each other. When you communicate constructively you leave little room for those relationship spoilers: "assumption" and "doubt." With clear communication, you both know where the other is coming from. Whenever a serious issue arises, talk about it.

Do not compete with any background distractions when you want to talk about something serious. Make sure the TV, radio, cell phones, and kids are all turned off. No one wants to pour their heart out only to repeat themselves, because

Maury was about to give the results to Sharon and Devon on paternity-test day. However, if a TV is on, do not turn it off yourself! I repeat, *do not turn it off*! He has to, in order to show you he is really interested in what you have to say at the moment. If you walk into a room and turn off a TV he was watching, because what you have to say is more important than anything he is watching, and no one has died or is in the hospital, you are making a tense situation worse. He, like a kid, will only think about the fact that you came in the room and interrupted his program. No matter if you think he is one or not, do not do that.But we all know that you can't talk to someone when they are not receptive. For this reason, I'm going to let you in on some tried and true man-tips.

Do not talk to a man when:
1. he is sleepy.
2. he is eating, unless you are asking him how the food tastes or would he like seconds or thirds.
3. he is playing PlayStation and tells you any old thing to shut you up.
4. he is horny, unless you want to talk about something freaky and kinky.
5. he is watching sports, unless you want to talk about sports.
6. he is on his way to work.
7. he walks through the door from work.
8. he is on an important phone call.

The best time to talk to a man is:
1. when he is done eating, but not laying down.

2. when he is walking through the mall.
3. right after church.
4. right before bed, if both of you are too tired for sex
   but not yet sleepy.
5. on a pay day.

The Strong Silent Type ······················

If you have followed my man-tips, and your man is still not communicating, you might have a man that is just not a talker or isn't good at articulating his feelings (and no, that is not part of the definition for "men" in the dictionary). In these situations, you have to be patient and spend more time listening than talking. Men who are not good talkers often talk in circles or go off on tangents. If you know your man has trouble communicating, do not use it as an opportunity to outtalk him or not let him get his point across. He will eventually feel that communication with you is pointless. If this is the case, your relationship is going downhill and in a hurry. He only will get frustrated and go do Lord knows what with a woman who is patient enough to listen.

How Do I Say . . . ? ························

When it comes to men, get right to the point. No need for fluff. He will like the directness and appreciate not guessing what is wrong with you. What irritates a man the most is a woman shutting down and wanting him to guess what is bothering her. Open your mouth and say something!

Why make an upsetting situation worse? If you cannot talk, because you need to calm down about something first, then that is understandable. But as soon as you are able to look at him without wanting to slap him, tell him what is on your mind.

And don't sugarcoat things trying to save his feelings. If you need help with cleaning up, finances, kids, car maintenance, his family, your family, *say so*. If he is the problem and is not doing what he said he'd do. *Say so*. Give him the chance to correct the situation, or address your grievance.

If you are not a good communicator yourself, letters always work. Every man can relate to mail. Sometimes if you can't say the words, it can be better to write them. You get your feelings out, and you don't have to worry about getting tongue-tied. If you go this route, make sure you are dating someone who can read.

The Bottom Line

Effective communication with your man does not mean the two of you will agree on everything. You *do not* have to agree on everything. It can't be your way or the highway, because if it is, date yourself! You are two separate people, so you should never expect someone to agree with you on everything, but what you should understand is that you two can disagree respectfully.

Ripped from Finesse's Own Journal ··········

So much of what I'm sharing with you comes from the experiences I've had, good and bad. Even now, although I'm in a solid relationship that makes me happier than I could have ever imagined, we have our moments. I'm good, but I ain't perfect, and I'm still learning. Read on.

After spending a great night role-playing, like we were at a house party (we flaked on an actual one we'd been invited to) the next day we had the biggest fight. It was ugly. How did it start? Don't remember. Why did it start? Don't know. Who started it? She did! That, I do remember. I am very good at remembering the important stuff, like who started fights and who won. And I was losing the argument bad. She was making me feel so small that I wanted to hide under the bed until the mean woman left the room.

She said I needed a change in my attitude. To her, everything lately has been about me— *my* career, *my* schedule, *my* money, *my* house, *my* "next thing." I felt like I'm working toward something better for both of us, but to her there has been no us. It has been all about me all the time.

I come home from the road, and my mind is still on the road. At times I'm too consumed with work. I'll stare off into space and just reflect on a gig, what went right, what went wrong, who I need to call, what I need to read, etc. When she wants to tell me something she is really hyped about, she says I seem disinterested. In fact, according to her, I don't even pretend to be interested. She's lying, I thought, but whatever. She was on a roll. Her mouth trembled. Her eyes welled with tears. Her nose began to run, and I couldn't make things better. It was the type of moment when even if I offered her a tissue, she would get more upset, because I was showing her I was more concerned about her runny nose than listening (I've learned a thing or two from past relationships). So I just sat there like a child in the principal's office.

Her beef? I hadn't been present. Sure, I was home, but I wasn't present. And she let me know how much it hurt her feelings.

Being in show business, it seems the harder I work to make something positive happen with my career, the thinner I spread myself and the more I have on my mind. But that's the case with any business or job that requires a lot of time and focus. I just figured no matter how you slice it, your personal life always suffers some. That's not how she figured it, though.

I lost the hell out of that argument, but after a while I didn't want to win. Sometimes guys say they're listening, but they don't really understand what's being said. Some men, like me, listen for pauses, so we can regain control of the conversation and finish the point we were trying to make before we were interrupted. But this time I got it. I realized she wasn't saying, "I am right, Finesse, and you are wrong." She was saying, "This is how I feel! Listen to me!" When someone cares for you as much as I know she cares about me, you gotta know when to shut up and make some instant adjustments. I know she has done a ton of it for me. Now it was my turn.

Her request was simple and valid. "When you come home from the road, *be* home. With me." I read once in a magazine where Lauryn Hill said, "Love is presence." I believe that 100 percent. How can you say you love them if you're never present to show it? I apologized to her, held her tightly, and was glad to have lost that argument.

Tit for Tat

Most people hate tit for tat. But men hate it with a passion. What *is* tit for tat?

"YOU KNOW WHAT . . ."

Naja enters the bedroom. Latisha is halfway under the covers. She is tying a scarf around her head.

Naja: Babe, what are you doing tonight?

Latisha: I am really tired. I think I am going to bed early.

Naja: Okay, well, I am going over to Barry's house to hang out. We might go out later for drinks at the W hotel.

Latisha: Okay, I might go out too. I think I am going to call Keisha and see what she is up to.

Naja: I thought you just said you were going to bed, because you were tired.

Latisha: I said I *might* go to bed early, because I was tired. But what's the big deal? You're going out, right?

Naja: Okay, whatever. (under his breath) You get on my nerves.

I just made this woman up in my head, but I already don't like her. So if her man said he was going to stay home also and reorganize the T-shirt drawer, would homegirl still call Keisha? Probably not. Okay, I am sure of it now. I do not like this fictitious girl.

Ladies, there is no need to feel like you need to match

your man's actions. If you want to go out, say that from the jump. If you would like your man to stay home and cuddle with you until you both drift off to sleep to a late-night episode of *Cops*, then say so. But if your man asks you if you have plans for the night and your answer is, "I'm really tired. I am going to bed," why would you suddenly get the burst of energy to jump up and find something to do, because your man is going to hang out?

Or worse, as he gets dressed to go out, you give him the silent treatment and huff and puff around the house the entire time, until he asks you what's wrong and you answer, "Nothing." But it's like pulling teeth for him to get you to say something, but you assure him that you are "just fine." After a while, dude doesn't even want to go out anymore, or if he does, he can't enjoy himself, and spends his night bashing you to his boy. And trust me, his boy will be no help and might make matters worse once he hears what happened. That's just the nature of men. Any opportunity we get to brag to a guy, who is in a relationship, about how our boring life of chasing women who don't want us is better than their lives, we will milk it just to make ourselves feel better.

Hype Group v. Support Group ················

Don't let outside influences chip away at your relationship. Know sound advice when you hear it, and don't be afraid to be your own woman! A hype group is a group of women who usually have nothing positive to say about what goes on in your relationship. They often encourage women in relationships to stand up for themselves regardless of whether they have been wronged or are in the wrong. For example, "Girl, if I was you, I wouldn't let him tell me to get out of the house, just because the house is on fire. I'm a grown-ass woman. I know fire when I see fire. He act like he afraid to get burned or something. He weak! Yo' man is weak! He just trying to tell you what to do. See, you need to listen to me. Men try and run thangs. And that's *all* men, girl. They just want to tell you what to do and boss you around. Tell him you know how to stop, drop, and roll!"

Hype-group women are determined to bring down even the strongest relationship. It's always the single women looking for a good man with the most "advice." Be careful! If your man doesn't like one of your girlfriends, it's probably for a good reason.

A *support* group is a group of women that try their best not to let you mess up a good thing. They try to befriend you and your man without crossing any lines. When you are right, they tell you to stand firm, but maybe approach it in a different way. When you are wrong, they tell you when you are trippin'. Sometimes you can be with your man for so long, you can take him for granted, or vice versa. That's when your support-group girlfriends step in and remind you how silly you two are behaving, and encourage you not to ruin a good thing. Besides, neither of you are "going anywhere." They don't encourage you to disrespect your man or make you feel guilty about always choosing your man over "them."

Check Your Baggage at the Door ··············

We've all got baggage, whether it's the residue from previous relationships or unresolved childhood issues. It's the *unchecked* baggage that can burden and destroy a fresh relationship. How can you enjoy your new thing when you're still dealing with past emotions and hurts? You're not being fair to him or yourself. Don't look at your current man while still thinking about your ex.

When we meet new people, we start comparing them to the person we used to date, even if the old person was a jerk. So the new person doesn't have a chance from the start.

Before you get into a new relationship, accept that you cannot get rid of everything bad so easily. Bad tends to stay with you and linger. Learn to accept the past and see it for what it is, accept it and grow from it. Do not take new people for granted when they are trying to love you the best way they know how. If you are not completely ready, ask for a little time if you like the guy. If he really likes you, and if he can determine that you are serious, he will wait. If you take too long, or appear to be stringing him along, he will bounce.

THE BREAK-UP CHART

Based on my scientific Fin-Diddy research, these are the reasons women break up with men and the reasons men break up with women.

Reasons Women Break Up With Men

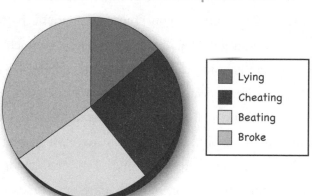

- Lying
- Cheating
- Beating
- Broke

Reasons Men Break Up With Women

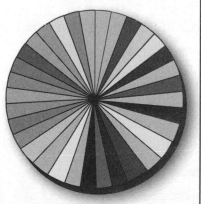

- Liar
- Shopaholic
- Trifflin' family
- Gaining too much weight
- Crazy baby-daddy
- Cheating
- Big Adam's apple
- Abusive
- Selfish
- No sex
- Bad sex
- Not enough sex
- Too confrontational
- One bad-ass kid too many
- Unplanned pregnancy
- Too needy
- Too jealous
- Too emotional
- Too critical
- We found someone else
- Too manipulative
- High maintenance
- Low maintenance
- Sloppy drunk in public
- Jheri curl
- Messy
- Crazy ex-boyfriend
- Nosey friends

The Irresistible Independent Woman! ········

Having too strong a sense of independence can also be baggage. Independence is good, but know that men like to feel needed or depended upon by their woman. Being independent and not needing a man is great, I guess, but stop getting into relationships waving the independent battle flag every chance you get. If you can do it all by yourself, pretty soon your man is going to wonder why he's there. If you feel that strongly about doing it solo, just stay single and continue to make your millions. But the minute you do decide to get into a relationship, realize that your man needs to feel like he's adding value to your life. I'm not saying make things up, but telling your man that no one takes out the trash, washes your car, really understands you, or makes you feel as good about yourself as he does, is not a bad idea.

R-E-S-P-E-C-T! ····························

Ever since Aretha shouted that back in the day, women have been demanding this from their men. But respect is a two-way street. Men don't expect their girlfriends to get on the back of motorcycles and go on a cruise with a guy friend (unless it has been proven beyond a shadow of a doubt that he is gay). That is disrespectful. And we also hate it when you do not introduce us to your guy friends who are attempting to play both of us. A man deserves the respect of being your man. If you feel like he only deserves your respect some of the time, then he should not be your man. Likewise, if you feel you are being disrespected, call him on it. If the disrespect continues, bounce. Without respect a relationship will not last.

Constructive Arguing ·······················

If this concept sounds like an oxymoron to you, it's probably because men usually associate the act of arguing as a heated, anger-filled tongue-lashing, when winning is all that matters. That first argument you have as a couple can be especially shocking and intense. When tempers flare, you each see a side of the other that you didn't know existed. Suddenly the sweet mouth that uttered loving words becomes twisted with rage. The decibel level of your voices rises, and lots of not-so-nice words spill out. He yells, because he thinks it helps him get his point across. You employ the classic black woman neck roll for extra emphasis when you have your say. You both become increasingly defensive, and go back and forth like this until one of you gives by leaving the scene, crying, or throwing something across the room. But you've both just spent a lot of time and emotion on a problem without solving it.

When you realize you love someone, arguing should not be about making someone feel stupid or belittled. It should not be about controlling someone, or winning an argument, or having them "in check." It's about peace. Even when you think you have someone in check, you really don't, and just know you are dating a very frustrated and unhappy person.

In an argument your main goal should be to listen and understand why your partner feels the way they do. You cannot be listening to someone if you are thinking about what you are going to say next. Often people yell and repeat themselves, because they don't feel really listened to. No one said, "I heard everything you said." No one said, "You have a good point." No one even bothered to say, "I disagree." The other person only started arguing their point, and was waiting for the person talking to shut up.

Arguments wouldn't last as long and get as loud if people really listened to one another. Do you often find yourself saying the same thing four different times, four different ways, each time getting louder? He is not listening. He is waiting to talk, because you said something he disagreed with. A man's brain will stop right at the moment you say something he believes is wrong. He's thinking, if you are going to yell, you should at least get everything right (which, of course, is impossible). That's why it's best to keep things blunt with men and wait for them to respond. The longer you draw out making a point, we only look for holes to jump in and out of, or get stuck on something irrelevant and make you repeat the last twenty minutes of what you'd just said.

Discussion Starters ·······················

When communicating with a man who seems to dance around issues or never "hears you," use direct questions followed by *silence*. Make your man respond directly to the problem. If he feels the need to defend himself, let him, but go right back to the very thing that is bothering you—no matter what he says. Make him address the question/ problem. Stay in control. If he gets upset, tell him there is no need to yell or get into a karate-kid position. Bring him back to the issue without turning the argument into something else.

There's a wrong and a right way to get the dialogue going. Here are two examples of what I'm talking about:

Michelle and Keedar both stare at a messy kitchen. Keedar is rubbing his belly and picks his teeth with a toothpick. There is a high-heel shoe on the floor next to the refrigerator, for no reason at all.

Scenario #1

Michelle: Time to bust them suds, Shawty. . . .
Keedar: I don't think so. The last time I cooked, I had to clean up, because you left the dishes and food out. You didn't do it last time.
Michelle: I *always* clean up around here. You don't

never do nothing but sleep and eat. Who do you think I am? Hazel?

Keedar: I don't know who you are, but if Hazel is around, tell her to come out here and pick up your raggedy Payless shoe by the refrigerator and put it somewhere before it ends up in the dishwasher with the rest of these dishes!

Scenario #2

Michelle: I cooked, and you said you would clean up. Do you mind taking care of the kitchen before we go to bed?

Keedar: Last time I cooked, I had to clean up, because you left the dishes and food out. I know if one person cooks, the other said they would clean, but you didn't do it last time.

Michelle: I'm sorry I did that. Would you like to knock it out together and start over fresh tomorrow?

Keedar: (shocked) Uh . . . okay . . .

Michelle: Thank you, babe. If you hurry up, there will be something waiting for you in the bedroom.

(Keedar gets up in a flurry of activity.)

This is an example of how a simple discussion could turn into an ugly fight. Keedar was probably waiting all week for her to cook, so he could remind her that she didn't clean up last time he cooked. In Scenario #2, she was heard and he was heard. She offered a compromise/solution. Because ultimately it's not about who cleans up after who. A fight was avoided.

Take Some Criticism ·······················

If your man is expressing a legitimate gripe about you, don't counter it with something from the past.

Men and women are both guilty of this, and it is not constructive at all. But I have noticed that women, especially black women, will get very used to telling black men what they are doing wrong. Why? Well, that's probably because we do a lot of things wrong (depending on your man). But the minute we tell you or bring to your attention that you are doing something wrong or hurtful, or have a behavior or an attitude that's problematic to us directly or the relationship as a whole, you counter it with bringing up all the negative things we do or have done. Men do it too, but women do that a lot. What he did in the past is in the past, and if you didn't bring it up then, now is not the time. You're not affirming his feelings by pointing out how yours have been hurt by something from two years ago. So, stop it!

Read and learn.

Skip and Olivia are a couple who lives together.

> Skip: Babe, can you please not have all the
> lights on in the house? If you leave a room, turn
> out the light.
> Olivia: Well, can you please not leave your
> clothes laying around everywhere?
> Skip: What clothes?
> (Olivia looks around the house. The house is spotless.)
> Olivia: Well, I don't see any right now, but you
> know how I am always picking up after you?
> (Skip shakes his head and leaves the room to
> avoid getting his third strike and facing serious
> jail time.)

Olivia was totally wrong. She never acknowledged what he said. She does not even say she will make an effort to stop leaving the lights on. She answered his complaint with a complaint of her own that was not even an issue at that very moment.

Cain't Tella Nuthin'! . . . .

Ladies, have you ever dated or lived with a man and had to tell him everything twice, or continually asked him to stop doing certain things that annoyed you? Then, out of the blue, days later, he told you to stop doing something, like . . . leaving bits of your hair all over the bathroom? Then you thought to yourself, *"He has some nerve!"* You have? See, that's a problem.

Think of it this way: a man may be slow in a lot of areas he never thought twice about. A woman realizes that in her process of learning and loving him with each passing day. But as they bond, she will slowly begin to correct her man more often, make him aware of more things he should care about (global warming, recycling, cats), or tell him to change things about himself outright ("Don't tuck your sweater into your pants ever again"). Most men already prepare themselves before they enter into relationships, because they know this metamorphosis is going to happen.

But some women get so used to pointing out things to their men, when *you* are the one actually told to make a change, you take it personally, or as payback or pettiness—not something valid or simply for what it is. It is a complaint. Try and make the one change he asks of you without huffin' and puffin'. Show him by example how you want him to respond when you tell him your list of everything you wish he would change for you.

Picture this:

JJ sits next to his girlfriend Dina. He looks very uncomfortable. He leans over and whispers to Dina.

> JJ: Can you not wear your jeans so low on your
> hips every time we go out?

❧

161

Dina: Why? Do I tell you what to wear?

JJ (still whispering): Actually, you do. All the
time. Yes.

Dina: Well, you didn't mind when you met me
wearing these jeans.

JJ (yelling): I'm just saying, babe. Damn, we in
church! (whisper) I'm sorry, Pastor.

Have you ever heard a woman say something, like, "You can't tell me *nothing*, because I know what I'm talking about." (And she really means it.) The subject can be kids, food, cars, nightclubs, country music, Biggie's death, Nevada, transmissions, birds, clouds, or insects. She is a damn expert on everything. But worse, she applies that attitude toward everything, especially dealing with her man.

I do understand that some men have too much to say or act the exact same way. But if you have a man that is pretty chill, laid-back, but he does his thang and is perfect for you, pay attention to how you react when he complains, offers a suggestion, or just brings something to your attention. If you are really bothered by something your man says to you, have a valid reason as to why.

On the Same Page? ·

You want kids, but he does not want any. You are pretty serious about a career change to belly dancing, but he is going into the ministry. You like to go out and be around a lot of people. He likes to stay in and hates strangers. You think the pig is the greatest gift God gave man, and he is thinking of changing his name from Terrance Rashad to Tyrick X.

A lot of times people are together for a while, and suddenly someone wants to make a turn in the relationship that the other does not agree with. They both feel very passionate about their positions. What do you do? Who is right and who is about to do something the other person did not sign up for?

It is great when people find themselves and discover something they think will bring them fulfillment. But if a man is heading in a certain direction, he will expect his woman to go that direction with him. For example, I like you, and I know you like me, but I go around and speak to kids for a living and ask them to stay off drugs and stay in school. You sell crack. I guess you gotta do what you gotta do, but if you want to get with me, no more selling crack to kids in the parking lot right after I give a speech. We are not on the same page.

Now, there are some men who are out there, and they have *no* plan. Their plan is whatever their woman thinks their plan should be. To each his own, but know the type of man you have and make sure you click with his overall personality. I think more relationships last longer when a man takes charge and says, "This is what I do, this is how

I roll, and this is where I am headed. Tell me how you need me to love you as you help me go in this direction. Can you make a happy life for yourself as we head in this direction? Is there any way I can help you do what you want to do as we head in this direction?" Some women might think that is old-fashioned. But couples with very different goals are usually the first to break up. And what's crazy is they knew they couldn't change each other before they even entered the relationship.

Everyone gets urges to go in new directions and try new things. That is just a part of living life. But two people in a relationship should flow together, with each person fulfilling their dreams and feeling pretty good about life. It's called "compatibility." Men should roll with their women, and women should roll with their men. *Get on the same page and pick a direction.*

The Power of Asking ·······················

Men feel like women do not ask enough questions or ask for help when they need it. Women either go silent and let something build up to the point that it creates an ulcer, or they go from zero to sixty in the middle of putting a noun and a verb together. If you yell, we yell. If you curse, we curse. Instead of all of that, just ask.

Asking brings a lot of clarity to a relationship. If you are confused about something, or just don't understand it fully, do not hold it in and do not go berserk. Just *ask*. Get the clarity and understanding you need for your peace of mind. Depending on the answers you get or don't get, *then* decide to hold it in or go berserk.

Men Hate Guessing

Do not make a man guess why you are upset with him. Men think that is dumb. Tell him why you are upset with him, and then decide to give him the silent treatment or to just put some space between the two of you. There is no point of two people being in the same room when one person is getting ignored and has no idea why. Asking what's wrong fifty times, only to be told "nothing" fifty times while you stick pins into a voodoo doll that looks remarkably like us is just not cool. Be mad, be upset, but let us know why, so we can at least begin the process of getting out of the doghouse.

Note: If your man already knows why you are upset, but acts like he doesn't, he is wrong. You then have the right to ignore him. It is very important to know the difference between a man asking, "Tell me what's wrong, so I will know what this is about" and "You mad?" (when he knows damn well that you are a tad "heated").

The Bottom Line

No relationship can last without compromise. It cannot be everybody just doing their own thing, or one person making all the sacrifices while the other person is sitting back, chilling. That builds resentment and breeds crazy people, because eventually somebody is going to snap!

However, do not compromise on anything you hold valuable. It will slowly destroy your relationship and you in time. You will turn around one day and realize everything you hold dear or think is important is gone. Meanwhile, the other person has not given up anything significant.

Relax, You Ain't Missing Nothing ············

Sometimes you get mad at your mate, because you feel like you are missing out on something by *having* a mate. You are not missing out. You have to realize fun and trouble are very close allies. A lot of single people cannot consistently enjoy the type of fun that people in good relationships possess. Remember, being in a relationship is a choice. If you feel like you can't honor the commitment and understanding you have with your mate, fortifying it with respect and consideration every time you are tested, then just be single. Some people rush to marry, and then turn around and say they regret not doing "this" or "that" before they got engaged. Be mature and don't let the feeling of missing out rip you apart or drive the person who loves you, crazy. If you have something good, don't be foolish by throwing it away for more games, more clubs, more people. It is absolutely not true about the grass being greener on the other side. In fact, it's that damn fence that most people have a problem with. We create our own walls. Remember that.

Separation Issues ··························

If you are in a relationship, learn to trust him, for your own peace of mind. Concern yourself with being the best you, and let your man focus on him. You cannot control him. He cannot control you. If he has never given you a reason to doubt him, then don't start. Don't fear your man going out without you. Don't question your man about everyone and everything.

If you don't trust your man, leave him. It is that simple. But if he has never given you a reason not to trust him, and you *don't* trust him, then you probably have insecurities and self-esteem problems. There are justified and unjustified suspicions. If you can never reach him by cell phone, and he always has lame excuses for his disappearing acts, or traces of other women are popping up all over the radar, then by all means confront him and handle your business. (But that does not mean spend every day playing detective. Everything is revealed sooner rather than later.) But if you have issues with him just doing things without you, then you may have separation issues and don't like to be alone. Fix that before you ruin your relationship.

There is no point making accusations and threats when all your man said was, "I'll be back." When? Where? What?

Who? How? and Why? are not necessary unless you are dating a child or you need to plan your schedule around his. Get the information you need for the obvious reasons, but don't make your man feel he cannot leave the house without you. That is not sexy at all.

The Bottom Line ·

In a relationship, you will grow as a couple and you will grow as an individual. Individual growth is often what scares people. When one person grows too much (professionally, financially, and socially), it makes the other person feel uneasy. We want to keep the person we love in a box— exactly the way we met them. In the beginning we love their independence and the fact that they have their own friends with their own lives. As we grow closer, we become more attached, and we fear their individual growth could possibly lead to change or separation. So we get more emotional, and more demanding, and more insecure about what could happen if we turn our backs for a second on the one we love. In our minds, our lover becomes "untrustworthy" and we feel the need to "protect" them from everyone, even themselves. But we only end up behaving like a nervous wreck, and we end up pushing away the one we love. Trust that your man loves you and he is with you because he wants to be.

CHAPTER EIGHT
on bended knee

Ladies, as I stated in the beginning I wrote this book with the sole intent of giving you a black man's perspective on dating and relationships. I've discussed the importance of being clear on who you are as a person and assessing what you want from a man and a relationship; given you strategies for approaching men you're interested in; shared some ideas on dating; given you my frank opinion on intimacy and sex; and offered solutions for some of the obstacles and difficulties that can creep up in love. I've given you more than my two cents on what men think about dating and relationships, but the one perspective I can't yet give you is that of a *married* black man. I'm not there yet, but I'm working on it.

Since the goal for many of you may be marriage, I turned to the experts: married men. I thought it would be cool to let them weigh in on their decisions on making honest women out of their girlfriends, and give you advice on finding a husband.

These brothas have stripped away all pretenses and bared their souls in an effort to help sisters around the world become as happily in love as they are. Well, not quite, but some of them possess a real romantic streak (wait till you read about how Wayne K. from Hartford, Connecticut, proposed to his wife). One thing's for sure: After reading these testimonials there's no denying that there are some good brothers out there—in love and loving the institution of marriage. Here's how they tell it:

Tony B.

Thirty-seven years old
Chicago, Illinois
Advertising executive
Married for eight years

When I proposed to my wife, it was a bit of a production, because I wanted it to be real special. I arranged a private dinner for her and her girlfriends at a popular restaurant in town. She didn't know it was a setup (her friends said they were all going to check out the new chef's cuisine). She enjoyed her meal so much that she asked to meet the chef at the end of dinner to tell him how great the food was. I came out dressed as the chef and got on one knee and proposed to her. The whole restaurant went crazy!

What women have to remember is, a cat will respect you

more if you stand your ground on your beliefs and what you want, but don't be too hard on him. Give him freedom to be who he is, but let him know that he's got to respect you in everything he does and every move he makes.

Stan B.

Thirty-five years old

Decatur, Georgia

Artist

Married for five years

You can marry anyone, so looking to get married is easy. But to make it worth your time and effort, you need to seek your soul mate—a person who knows you inside and out, who thinks your flaws are endearing, whom you can call your best friend, who believes in all your dreams and desires. When you marry your soul mate you get a lasting union to match all your highest hopes.

Two years into our relationship I popped the question. We were sitting on the couch, eating hot dogs and drinking champagne on a random Thursday night (random to her, but not to me). It was before the long Memorial Day week-end, and she had suspicions I was going to propose. We'd booked a hotel room near a local park, so we could walk back and forth from the annual jazz festival there and have a little vacation from our daily lives.

Since I wanted the proposal to be a surprise, and figuring she would be expecting something during the weekend, I popped the question a day early, in a most unusual setting. After cooking up that culinary treat of Hebrew National beef hot dogs, I put the ring in a glass of champagne and brought it out to her with the food. She went through a couple of bites of her hot dog and a few sips of champagne before noticing the ring in the glass. Once she discovered it, she was speechless, then cried. In fact, I wasn't quite sure she'd said yes and had to ask her again to be sure—not that there was any doubt she would. We still have the hot-dog package as part of our scrapbook. The proposal fit our personalities: nontraditional, a little strange, but effective.

Roderick B.
Twenty-six years old
San Diego, California
Executive recruiter
Married for two years

After dating my wife for the last two weeks of our senior year of high school, I changed my choice for college and showed up at hers in the fall. We dated for six years, and I proposed after four, but I knew from the start she'd be my wife.

Once I decided to propose, I had our former high school English teacher call her in to fill out a survey about her former students who went into education (my wife is a teacher). She arrived on a Saturday, sat in our old classroom, and began to fill out the survey, which was a bogus one I'd concocted. It actually contained questions pertaining to our relationship. I organized my family and hers outside of the classroom door. When I got the signal from our teacher, I walked in dressed up to the nines in a suit with flowers in hand and twenty family members following me. At first she asked, "What are you doing here? And why do you have a suit on?" After she saw our family, and I got down on one knee, she got it. I told her that I wanted to ask her to marry me in the place where our love first began. She was completely blown away.

Ladies, don't let men string you along, because some of us will do just that. Draw a line in the sand and make a choice. I always heard my grandmother say this to the women in my family: "Why would he buy the cow, when he get milk for free?" So true.

Clark D.

Thirty-two years old
New York, New York
Corporate director
Married for two and a half years

I asked my wife to marry me in about a foot of snow on a quiet night in Central Park. At first she wouldn't stop talking

long enough for me to ask. She kept going on and on and on about the weather. I thought for a moment I was about to propose to Al Roker. Finally I just got down on one knee and asked. To say she was shocked would be an understatement.

She and I were friends in college, where we had a class together. I was walking home from campus as she was walking to the campus. She was wearing a T-shirt, shorts, and a gigantic backpack that looked like it was filled with every book she owned. She held a water bottle in one hand and a cell phone in the other, talking to her mom. She stopped to say hi, and I asked jokingly, "Do you even know where the library is?" She laughed, said good-bye, and as I walked away I heard her say, "No, Mom, I swear I know where the library is. It's the tall building." At that exact moment I realized that this was who I wanted to marry. I'm not sure how I knew, I just did. We dated for three years before we got married, though.

In my opinion, men should wait as long as they can without losing the girl.

WHY BLACK MEN WAIT SO LONG TO GET MARRIED

Q: How come many black men don't marry until they're in their thirties, but white guys are ready to walk down the aisle in their early twenties?

I have often pondered that same question. White guys do seem to get married earlier than black guys. In fact, are black guys still getting married? Of course we are, but I personally don't know why anyone in their early twenties would want to settle down with anyone for the rest of their lives. While I was in college, I saw plenty of white guys fall in love and marry their college sweethearts a year after graduation. Black guys were just trying to graduate on time.

I believe in marriage, and I think it definitely enhances your life when you find that right someone. But black men in their early twenties are probably some of the most confused humans walking Earth. Black men need time to grow up mentally and socially. We know nothing in our early twenties other than we think we are invincible and the world owes us something. I think making a big commitment, like marriage, at twenty-three is suicide (by that same logic, I'd also advise against an "I love Yo-Yo" tattoo on your chest). Black men change their minds way too much in their early twenties, and black women don't stick around long enough for their soul mate to figure himself out.

Statistics have shown that those early marriages don't last too long. Now, I don't actually know where that data can be found, but I know it is reported some-where each month. I mean, maybe getting married early was the thing to do back during *The Color Purple* days, but a lot of single black men in their early twenties will tell you that marriage is the last thing on their minds in today's world.

When I was growing up, my father always told me to wait until I was thirty to marry (he also claimed marriage stunts your growth and makes you go bald). He said that a man is like a nice sports car, and when you get married too early, it's like putting a boot on your own tire. "Don't put a boot on your car, son." I think what he was trying to tell me is that young men don't know themselves in their early twenties, and it's hard to make a commitment to someone else when you don't know yourself yet. Maybe white guys don't get the same advice about marriage that black guys get, but I do know that we eventually get tired of driving the sports car, with no one in the passenger seat.

Samuel F.

Forty-three years old
Philadelphia, Pennsylvania
Attorney
Married for three years

Early in our relationship my wife had me over to help her hang curtains. It was then that I noticed we worked real well together. We talked and drank tea, and the chemistry was so strong; we really could have been doing anything. That's when I knew she was the one for me. A few months later she was in the kitchen one morning, wearing a robe, when I got down on one knee and asked her to marry me.

Women should think more like men. Instead of thinking about what a man thinks or what will make a man happy. Figure out what and who is going to make *you* happy. As young girls, many of you watched your mother pamper and please your father, so that's where that bad habit started. Instead, prepare a list of what will make you happy. But it shouldn't include superficial things, like he needs to be six feet tall, make at least twelve dentist trips yearly, drive only German cars produced on the western side of Germany, have PEP (Potential Earning Power), well-manicured nails— you get the idea!

Finally, know and like yourself because if you don't have your own house in order, we will know. We're very intuitive that way. In my experience, women who have a strong religious foundation, a significant family support system in place, or are generally very secure, give off the most positive vibes. I realize there is a shortage of good men out there; however, there are pockets of good men. You just have to be a cunning hunter!

Wayne K.

Thirty-three years old
Hartford, Connecticut
Pediatrician
Married for four years

We had been friends throughout medical school, but the moment it turned into more than friendship and I started kissing her, I knew I would marry her.

I planned months in advance to propose to her. I wanted everything to be memorable. We arranged a trip to Napa Valley, California, and stayed with her family out there. They have a beautiful house overlooking the entire valley. After asking her parents for permission, I called her aunt and uncle and told them of my plan. They recommended a winery with fantastic wine and an amazing location as a good place to pop the question. (Joseph Phelps Vineyards was reluctant to allow me to use their private picnic area without being a member of their wine club until I told them that I intended to propose to my girlfriend there.)

The winery blocked out the entire area for us, and we had a nice picnic lunch, a bottle of wine, and then I popped the question. After she said yes, we went to a spa for the rest of the day before heading to the French Laundry for dinner. I ate the best meal of my life on the happiest day of my life. What a day!

Anyone can get married, but I think in order to be happily married, you have to love and appreciate each other's true inner being. Who knows? Maybe I'm just a big sap, but I'm a happy big sap.

Richard V.

Forty-five years old
Cleveland, Ohio
Publicist
Married for twenty years

As soon as I saw my wife moving into the dorm, I told my boys, "Stay away from her, that's my wife!" We lived together for five years, first, and then we decided to go for the whole thing. Living together was crucial, because you have to know the person you are supposed to spend the rest of your life with. We might have been living in sin, but divorce is worse!

If you're in a relationship and want to get married, ask straight up. Wife did. After we lived together for four years she asked, "Are we going to get married?" That got me thinking, *Is my life better with her in it?* The answer was simple—yes! If you don't get the right feeling in the gut from his response, then, as painful as it sounds, bounce!

If you're looking for the right man go to places that you normally would go. Don't worry about going alone.

Auctions, the opera, theater, museums, art galleries, benefits for causes you believe in, car shows . . . Visit different churches other than your own. Going to the club is not where you are going to meet your future husband. You will meet men, no doubt, but in the club we are not looking for wife-y. If you see someone who interests you, approach him—don't wait for him. Ask all the questions you want to know the answers to; like, if he's in a relationship or if he is married. You don't want any surprises later.

Bill T.

Thirty-nine years old
Los Angeles, California
Corporate CEO
Married for eighteen months

My wife and I got engaged exactly six months after we met. I proposed to her at her parents' fortieth anniversary celebration the day after Christmas, so it was all very special.

To all the women looking for husbands, stop looking! We can sense when you are looking. Just live right, keep God first, and he will supply all of your needs. Be *you*, not who you think we want you to be. If you have to drastically change who you are to fit in with a man, he probably isn't the right one for you.

Ahmed L.

Forty-six years old

Oakland, California

High school guidance counselor

Married for three years

Since this is my second marriage (I was married sixteen years the first time around), I'm much more attuned to being a good husband and not just a good father. After four months of dating my wife, I had that feeling that goes way back to adolescence—butterflies and all! I waited about eight months before asking her to commit to our relationship, because it was necessary for me to meet her family and establish bonds with them.

One of the books that she cherishes is called *A Wrinkle in Time*, and I had not read it. To better understand her, I read the book and took thorough notes, which formed a love letter that I wrote to her. I proposed to her when she returned from a weekend with her girlfriends that started on the wrong foot. It caught her off guard when I gave her the letter and proposed with a watch instead of a ring. Actually, I gave her two watches, and so it was symbolic of her favorite book and our relationship.

All you single women looking to get married, keep the faith; maintain high standards, but have realistic expectations of relationships; and prepare to give a little.

Paul B.
Fifty-one years old
New York, New York
IT manager
Married for thirty years

Don't be in a hurry to get married. Be patient and wait until you find who you want, not who you'll settle for.

Tony J.
Fifty years old
Ridgefield, Connecticut
Public relations executive
Married for twenty-four years

I was on the eighteen-month plan for getting married: We dated for eighteen months, got engaged for eighteen months, and got married eighteen months later. I popped the question on Christmas Eve, in our apartment.

My suggestion to women who want to be married is to first be happy. Then marry the person who makes you happy. Marriage is an arrangement. Happiness is a state of being.

Leonard T.

Forty-two years old

Charlotte, North Carolina

Nurse

Married for seventeen years

My wife and I were college sophomores together, then reunited three years after our initial meeting, and dated seriously for three years before getting married. About eleven months after we started dating, I knew we should get married. It was after she relocated from D.C. to New York City to start her career. The long-distance relationship was tough right from the start.

She had gone out of town on business for a few days. The night she came back, I made her dinner. It was nothing out of the ordinary, because I often cooked for us. We had wine with our dinner, so when she wasn't looking I dropped the ring in her wine glass. The next time she picked up her glass, she saw it. Guess she could have choked on the ring, so might not have been the best idea. We laugh about it still today. I thought it was romantic at the time, though.

I hear a lot of women say they're looking for a husband. I say stop looking. Sounds clichéd, but the right man for you is probably the one you least expect it to be.

Herbert A.

Fifty-one years old
Detroit, Michigan
Attorney
Married for twenty-five years

My wife was washing dishes at my kitchen sink when I gave her a dozen roses. In the box with the roses, I placed the box with her engagement ring.

The best advice I can give young women is to make sure you're willing to work through everything with your man—the good, the bad, and the ugly. Make sure your man is willing to do the same.

Jonathan P.

Thirty years old
Los Angeles, California
Event travel specialist
Married for one and a half years

They way I popped the question to my wife was during a small birthday party for myself, at a restaurant. I invited her friends and mine. When I blew out the candles, I staged for my friends to ask me what I wished for. I replied, "Let's see if it comes true," then I got on my knee and proposed.

Do not compromise yourself to get married. What God has for you, he has for you in his own time, not yours.

Steven N.
Forty-five years old

Alexandria, Virginia

Human resource specialist

Married for twelve years

My wife and I made plans to get married after having a discussion about it in an apartment we shared in Pittsburgh. We both decided it was the next step in our life together.

Conversation in a relationship is important. You have to be able to articulate your feelings and perceptions with your partner. Be yourself, and do not try to change the person you are with, but look to see if the person is developing and moving forward in his life.

Mark R.
Forty-three years old

Jacksonville, Florida

Financial advisor

Married for five years

I married my wife a year after we began dating. After six months we went on a Skyline Cruise. I took her to the top deck and surprised her by proposing.

Women who are looking to get married need to be a little

bit more flexible with whom they date. It shouldn't always be about how much money he has, but about who he is as a person. Is he ambitious? How much integrity does he have? What is this person's family background and does his belief system complement your own? When my wife and I first got married, she was making a lot more money than I was and also owned her home. This did not matter to her at the time, because she wasn't materialistic. She continues to believe in and encourage me, even when I don't deserve it.

Now, five years later, I have my own firm, mostly due to my wife's encouragement, love, support, and a lot of hard work. This is why married couples, who may have very little in the beginning, finish big in the end.

Finesse's Sum-up ···························

Represent, fellas! These married men of all ages and backgrounds just told you not only what got them to the altar, but what keeps them in their marriages. Some of them tied the knot after several years of knowing their wives. Others married quickly, but were no less serious and sincere about the commitment they were making.

And did you notice that a lot of the things they said, like knowing yourself, not compromising your standards, communicating, flexibility, not limiting your options, having a list, being realistic about your expectations, and not jumping into a relationship for the sake of having a man, echoed many of the points I already made? See, I know what I'm talking about. Take what we say to heart, ladies, and let it be your guide to the kind of love you want.

Along with giving you advice and tips on ways to forge and maintain a relationship with a black man, I've enjoyed sharing aspects of my own love life and the lessons I've learned from my dating experiences. As I mentioned, I haven't taken that trip to the altar yet, but as I've put the finishing touches on this book, there's been a major development in my relationship and life. I got engaged to my girlfriend, and we're planning our nuptials. Now, as an almost-married man, I'd be remiss if I didn't tell you how *I* proposed. Get comfortable and read on.

The Proposal ·

Jessica and I have been dating for almost two years and living together for nine months. We've created a beautiful home, filled it with all the comforts we enjoy, and play parents to three lively dogs. Most of all we've developed a solid, loving partnership that I feel will only get better with time. I'd decided that Jess was the woman for me, and now it was time for me to let her know it.

For her birthday she wanted to head to Orlando to celebrate with family and friends. She also wanted to see her all-time favorite rap artist, Nas, who'd be performing in the area. I thought this would be the perfect time—and event—to propose.

I'd met Nas at a celebrity charity event hosted by our mutual friend, Chris Webber of the Detroit Pistons. When I told Web of my plans to propose and my desire to do so at the concert, he immediately put me in touch with Nas. I hoped I wouldn't be putting Nas on the spot with such a major request, but married man that he is, he was totally cool and unbelievably accommodating.

Jess and I arrived at the House of Blues and got in backstage without a hitch. After making sure she was comfortable, I excused myself to review the plan with Nas. It was then that he let me know that MTV would be taping the entire thing for his new reality show. *"Really?"* I asked, trying to play it cool and not let this new fact unnerve me from the task at hand. But all I could think was, *Oh* snap. *If she says no, it will be aired on national television!*

The concert started, and Jess and I stood alongside of the stage, watching Nas perform his classics as the crowd went crazy. Before I knew it, he was performing his hit "Can't Forget About U." The proposal was to go down directly after that song. When it was over, he looked at me, while shouting into the mike, "Orlando, I normally don't share my stage with no one, but this next guy is a real dude. . . ." I didn't hear much else after that but my name. He handed me the mike, and I greeted the crowd with, "What's up, O-Town!" The way they screamed, you would have thought I was about to bust a rhyme.

I called Jess over, and she slowly took the stage, not quite knowing what to expect. Once she got settled on a stool that was brought out for her, I told the audience, "My girlfriend thinks she's here for her birthday, but actually . . ." I pulled out the ring box and held it behind my back. Folks went crazy! Nas pushed me down on one knee, and I looked at her and said, "I've never been more sure about anything in my life. Will you marry me?"

Then . . . silence! It was the longest four seconds of my life. She just stared at me, in shock. "Well?" I asked, holding my breath. "Yes! Yes! Yes!" she replied all at once. The crowd screamed, she cried, and I pulled her offstage, excited and relieved. The concert continued while Jess and I cried like babies backstage. It was a fantastic night and a memorable start to the next phase of our life together. When Jess and I are old and gray, this will be one of those moments we'll tell our grandkids about.

epilogue

Whatever you know about relationships and whatever your personal experiences have been, dealing with us men, I hope I've provided you with a little more insight from one man's perspective that you just can't get from your girlfriends. When a girlfriend tells you all men are the same, she has no clue what she is talking about. What she should say is that all the men *she* has dated were the same. You don't have to make her same mistakes.

So there you have it, ladies. I have just given you nearly two hundred pages of serious and not-so-serious suggestions on how you can realistically proceed on the path toward finding your man and knowing what and *what not* to do with him once you've got 'im. I hope that what I've told you throughout this book has been entertainingly (is that even a word?) helpful.

Moreover, I hope that my suggestions, advice, observations, and insight will eliminate any fear, anxiety, or apprehension you may have had about ever finding the right guy. If you are tired of people telling you to be patient, I understand, so I will be different. Here goes . . . Be *real* patient! (Hey, I tried.) The one for you is definitely out there. In the meantime, read the book again. The more you know and think like we think before we even think about what you think we are thinking, the better. I want you to feel empowered to attain the kind of healthy, happy relationship you deserve.

And truthfully I really hope you enjoyed reading my first book and having some good laughs. I love to leave people smiling.

Sincerely,

Your brother from another mother,

One Love.

Finesse Mitchell

about the author

FINESSE MITCHELL was a cast member on NBC's *Saturday Night Live* from 2003–2006. He is now headlining the best comedy clubs on the circuit and released his first stand-up comedy DVD, *Snap Famous*, produced by Quincy Jones' son, QD3. He also contributes a monthly dating-and-relationship column to *Essence* magazine.

Visit him online at www.finessemitchell.com and www.myspace.com/finessemitchell2.